HOW TO

BE A WRITER

THE DEFINITIVE GUIDE TO GETTING PUBLISHED AND MAKING A LIVING FROM WRITING

SALLY O'REILLY

piatkus

D0233569

PIATKUS

First published in Great Britain in 2011 by Piatkus
This paperback edition published in 2013

A CIP catalogue record for this book
is available from the British Library.

ISBN 978-0-7499-5405-5

Typeset in Baskerville BT by Palimpsest Book Production Ltd,
Falkirk, Stirlingshire
Printed and bound in Great Britain by
Clays Ltd, St Ives plc

Papers used by Little, Brown are from well-managed forests
and other responsible sources.

MIX
Paper from
responsible sources
FSC   FSC® C104740
www.fsc.org

Piatkus
An imprint of
Little, Brown Book Group
100 Victoria Embankment
London EC4Y 0DY

An Hachette UK Company
www.hachette.co.uk

www.piatkus.co.uk

Acknowledgements

I would like to thank Fay Weldon and the other writers and industry experts who contributed their words of wisdom so very generously to this book. Also my agent Judith Murray and Zoe Goodkin at Piatkus for their suggestions and sound advice and Celia Brayfield for believing in this idea from the start.

And a special thank-you to Noel, for help beyond the call of duty with double buggies, brainstorming and Being a Writer.

Contents

Foreword

Congratulations! You have published your first book. You can legitimately call yourself a writer. The book may even have been a great success, though the odds are, like most things, that the outcome will be neither as good as you hoped nor as bad as you feared. But, now the euphoria has faded, the adrenaline seeped away, now what? Where are the books that tell you how to *be* a writer? You need one. Your status in the world has somehow changed, and you feel it. Being this new person is going to take up a lot of your time, you can see, and you could do with some help.

How far can you trust the people you are now involved with? People want to interview you, but how do you control an interview? *Can* you? Is it bad form to ask for sales figures? (Your publisher certainly sounds as if it is.) There are dozens of books on the market telling you *how* to write, but none telling you what to do once you've proved that you can. You find you are on your own, playing it by ear.

It's a minefield, this business. How does the relationship between agent and writer, agent and publisher, work? Is it reasonable for the agent to charge the percentage they do? Should you press for a better deal? Do you have to have an agent at all? Do you grant the publisher world rights? What about film rights? Then there's the publicity round. Interviews, literary lunches, tours abroad, festivals – all have their own etiquette, their own rituals. By the time you get round to asking your PR person, she (it's usually a she) will be fully occupied with the next book on her list, and you feel silly asking for details. You feel vaguely that you ought to know already. Only you don't. Suppose you get up to read and realise you've forgotten your glasses. (Answer, ask someone in the audience to lend you theirs. There's always someone who will, and they'll like you the more for this show of ordinary human inefficiency.) What do you do if your books don't turn up at the festival? They're charging people to listen to you; how come you don't get paid? And so on. You tell a journalist something off the record and they publish it. Can you sue? Or will you never work again if you do? The publishers send you a bill for your launch party. Can they do this? It's all there in the contract, but you signed without reading it, more fool you. And so on.

Becoming a writer is one thing; *being* a writer is another. This is the excellent, informative book I should have been able to read, long ago and far away, when I was first published, to tell me how it was done, what to expect and how to get it right. *How*, in fact, *To Be a Writer*. All there now, at last, on the page, this new writer's handbook of etiquette and practicalities. Thank you, Sally O'Reilly, sincerely and truly.

Fay Weldon
March 2010

To Be or Not to Be . . .

There is one sure-fire way to be a writer, and that is to write. A lot. Every day if possible. When you feel like it and – even more important – when you don't. In that sense, there is absolute clarity about what being a writer means. But, in fact, many authors with published books to their names hardly find time to write at all. And thousands of people are scribbling away on a daily basis who would never say 'I am a writer' in case it sounds like showing off.

'Real' writers – such as Ernest Hemingway and Emily Brontë – have a mythic status. Intense, brooding, troubled, high-maintenance, maybe even suicidal. It's all part of the territory. Famous authors such as J. K. Rowling and Dan Brown are as renowned for their wealth as they are for their words. Few of us will achieve the mythic status of Hemingway or Brontë, or the bank balance of Rowling or Brown. But that doesn't mean that we aren't writers.

So what is this thing, this 'being a writer'? Publication helps, as does hard work, commitment, bloody-mindedness and talent, probably in that order. It's not a career, there is no neat progression from one level to the next, and you may find yourself 'hot' one year and forgotten the next. Being a writer is, in the old adage, 'a labour of love'. Writers are writers because they are compelled to write, no matter what the chances are of getting published. You are reading this book because you are one of this stoic, secretly determined breed. I am writing it because I'm one too, and I've learned to sustain my writing life the hard way.

I've been writing, on and off, since I was eight years old. I've been a journalist, a copywriter and an editor. And I've written poetry (really, really terrible poetry) and short stories (some of which won prizes) and published novels. I've had tremendous highs – I kept my editor's voice message telling me how much she loved my first book on my phone for months – and terrible lows. Rejection sucks, no matter how you look at it.

My experience has made me realise that writing is the easy bit. Much as we like to rant and rave about the difficulties of getting the words onto the page or screen, thoroughly as we may dust behind the radiators before we start, this is the aspect of the writing life that we control. The rest is dependent on the whims and judgements of others. To make your writing into any kind of living, any kind of way of life, you must address this. You must learn to sell your work, without feeling you are selling yourself. You must learn to deal with industry professionals, accountants, nay-saying friends and family, the daily grind. (You will probably have to learn to live with your day job, even after your book is in the bookshops.) You must overcome your inner critic, and ignore the outer ones. Above all, you must keep writing, keep believing in the importance of what you do, keep the faith.

In doing this myself, I have discovered not only that I am more hardworking, committed and bloody-minded than I thought I was, but also that I am a better writer. When my career seemed to have reached an impasse, I returned to first principles, thought hard about my craft, studied, taught, learned. I'm not famous now, and perhaps I never will be. But I have found a way to hard-wire writing into my life, and in doing this I have found meaning, purpose and that most elusive modern emotion: happiness. I hope this book will help you do the same.

CHAPTER ONE

So What Is a Writing Career?

'This before all: ask yourself in the quietest hour of your night: must I write? Dig down into yourself for a deep answer. And if this should be in the affirmative, if you may meet this solemn question with a strong and simple, I must, then build your life according to this necessity.'
Rainer Maria Rilke

If the number of 'how to write' books on the market is anything to go by, we should all be producing works of genius. The shelves of bookshops groan with guides to writing novels, short stories, radio plays, TV comedy and blockbusting Hollywood scripts. The three-act structure, the art of writing dialogue, developing character, starting to write, getting original ideas – it's all there. For the budding novelist, help is at hand for every stage of the process, from scribbling something illegible in a notebook to writing 'The End' when you think you may have reached it.

This is good news, up to a point. In the past, writers have had to work most of this out for themselves. The problem with this surfeit of how-to-write tomes is that most of these focus on the writing process, with the prospect of publication seen as the blessed reward for the chosen few. Those who are good enough will be allowed through the Pearly Gates, into the Heaven that lies beyond. (Any author who has visited

Penguin's palatial offices in the Strand will know what this feels like.) To some extent, a sense of euphoria is justified if you are Chosen. There is no doubt that only a tiny minority of wannabe writers find a publisher and that there will always be huge numbers of people who want to achieve this, and who will be disappointed. Finding a publisher is not only the defining career stage for authors, a coming-of-age as a professional writer, it is also an apparent recognition of exceptional talent.

But what happens once the mighty finger has pointed from the sky, rightly selecting You as the special one? All too often, the career plan ends there. The assumption is that getting published is like marrying the handsome prince at the end of a fairy tale – a happy ending. In fact, it's a new beginning; all that has ended is your time as an unpublished, unchosen writer. So is life from then on just a giddy round of metropolitan accolades and chilled Prosecco? Invitations to swap *bons mots* with Mark Lawson on BBC Radio 4? Dinner dates with Zadie Smith? Working holidays in Provence, during which you craft your Booker-winning tomes?

The answer is no. You have had a book published, and that is all. In 2010, more than 130,000 people in the United Kingdom had the same experience. For you, this is the fulfilment of a lifelong dream. For everyone else, it is of no more interest than an office promotion. In fact, one of the unspoken truths about getting published is that nothing happens at all. If you are lucky, you will see your book for sale somewhere. There may even be a small display in the window of your local bookstore. It's possible, though by no means certain, that your publisher will take you out for lunch. After that, the earth will continue on its axis, bus routes will remain unchanged, the items on *Newsnight* won't mention this new star in the publishing firmament, even your own mother will fail see the significance of what has taken place. The indifference of humanity will be inexplicable, but crushing. And, in the years that follow, expect the worst and you may be pleasantly surprised. Remember, even Martin Amis has had his ups and downs.

Writing For a Living – The Reality Check

By and large, writers are insecure, neurotic, introspective, solipsistic, egocentric and terrible with money. These are aspects of the authorial personality that will remain with us for life, whether we are sitting smugly at the top of the *New York Times* best-seller list or sharing the fifty-seventh chapter of a mind-altering space opera with our catatonic writing circle. Therefore, our problems stay with us, long after we have signed that first book deal.

Publishing is a tough business. It comes as a shock to many sensitive writers that executives in this line of work are just as interested in the bottom line as those who are selling mobile phones or mortgages. And it's much harder to isolate what makes a book sell. Developing a new iPhone or mortgage tracker deal will almost certainly shift some product, commissioning a new police procedural may not have the same effect. It's very tempting to see this as a regrettable feature of the modern world. Once upon a time, the story goes, people in publishing were all rather nice, wore a lot of tweed and took tea with Cyril Connolly. No one was terribly bothered about books making money as long as they were Literature, or somehow added to the gaiety of nations. Perhaps these people were a tiny bit stuck-up, but in a good way. They were forever nipping in and out of each other's Dickensian office in the streets of Bloomsbury, living the life of perpetual Oxbridge students: the Life of the Mind. Whereas nowadays it's all about TV tie-ins and celebrity memoirs, and hard-faced girls in designer black, and sober deals in Soho, and no one will care how brilliant your book is unless they have already heard of you.

Seeing modern publishing in this light is what psychologists call 'awfulising'. If you want to write, you are choosing a life that is both challenging and rewarding, and it was ever thus. While it is true that the spate of mergers and acquisitions that changed the face of publishing in the 1980s and 1990s was the beginning of a new, more ruthless era in the book business, this does not mean that writers had an easier time of it in the past. Traditionally, most writers have earned relatively little for their work, and authors who earn vast sums have always been the exception, not the rule. Indeed, one reason that writing has remained a middle-class occupation is that it has paid very poorly. A private income can make it easier to manage on a minuscule advance and tiny sales.

But in the twenty-first century the popular view is that – if you have the talent – writing books brings fortune as well as fame. It's as if we had no other way of measuring success. Along with this goes the strange belief that any money made from book sales is more like a lottery win than a pay slip for a proper job. When I got my first book deal I was paid £40,000 for two books. Given that it took me two years to write each one, this worked out at £10,000 a year – hardly a dizzying sum. In fact, if you divided this by the number of hours I slaved over each novel, I was working below the national minimum wage. Yet the reaction I had from friends and acquaintances was that this was jamminess of the first order. The head teacher at my daughter's school buttonholed me at parents' evening saying, 'Forty grand! Not bad, eh?' Heads swivelled. I think the other parents expected to see me kitted out in diamonds and floor-length leopardskin like Jackie Collins.

Somehow, the unknown author with a lower income than a nursery nurse is associated with a best-selling thriller writer with a vintage-car habit. Or, inevitably, with J. K. Rowling, the woman who has single-handedly done more to distort the public perception of writers' earnings than any other human being. (Through no fault of her own, it must be said.) Rowling's meteoric career is the stuff of folklore: she wrote the first Harry Potter book in penury and was rich by the time her second book came out. So she has become the benchmark. ('Writing a book are you? Maybe it'll be the next Harry Potter!') In this context, anything less than becoming a millionaire as the result of your labours looks like failure. And, in a society in which celebrity is everything, it seems as though we should all be chasing this goal to prove ourselves.

But that would be crazy. One of the great rewards of writing is being able to free yourself, and escape into a world of imagination and invention. Another is that your words can give your readers a similar means of escape. At its highest level, fiction can change lives, champion the underdog, carry a torch for free speech. Money and success? Ask most published writers what motivates them and few will talk about their earnings – or *OK!* magazine.

The Non-Millionaire Writer

What do we mean when we say 'career'? In most fields, a 'career' has come to mean a job for life, in which there is progress, development, security and – ideally – some degree of respect for experience and knowledge. Writing is a career only in the sense that it can last a lifetime. There is no career ladder, no pension scheme, no training or professional development or golden handshake at the end. Ironically, the rest of the employment market is rapidly catching up with this. You may even have bought this book following redundancy and with a view to replacing your old career with a new one. If so, you need to set your own goals and make your own provisions for old age – writing will not do it for you. And yet it is still a wonderfully rewarding and life-enhancing profession.

From Mrs Gaskell to Stevie Smith, from Daniel Defoe to Blake Morrison, writers have been characterised not by wealth and leisure, but by living busy lives and working hard. Where would we be without the non-millionaire writer? It is simply not true that those who have produced the greatest work are those who had the most time at their disposal. 'Ah,' you say, 'but the point is that money buys you time!' This is true in theory, but cast your mind back to the periods in your life when you have had the most time and freedom. Were you at your most productive? I know I wasn't. When I was an Eng. Lit. student at Goldsmith's College, it took me all day to eat a bowl of bran flakes and do the *Guardian* quick crossword. There was just no way I could fit in a Shakespeare seminar as well. Even now, the people I know who are most creative and inventive aren't those with the most time, or the most money. And successful authors fall into this category: if one day you are as well known as Bill Bryson or Hilary Mantel, you will be deluged with invitations and requests for your time. One of the skills that successful writers need to develop is that of keeping up with the writing itself, and not letting other demands take precedence.

Indeed, having long stretches of time to write can be a problem in itself. Reality recedes, and insanity beckons. Here is the late Beryl Bainbridge, talking about her writing life in *The Agony and the Ego*, a collection of interviews with writers compiled by Clare Boylan (Penguin, 1993):

> When I had a house full of children I used to think it would be wonderful to have the place to myself and all the peace I needed to write. Now I realize that it is so much easier to deal with frustrations of everyday life than to have to face oneself all day long. I live like a recluse.

I sometimes have cravings for this kind of privacy and isolation, and the thought of this semi-mythical house in Camden, in which a lone woman writes her weird fictions, is a symbolic place to me, a sort of Lost Domain. Not just a room of one's own, but a whole house! Dream on. (Paradoxically, it was Bainbridge's literary reputation that enabled her to live this hermit-like existence.) And yet this degree of isolation wouldn't suit everyone, and, as Bainbridge herself pointed out, much of her writing was produced in very different circumstances.

A Room of One's Own?

It was Virginia Woolf who specified that a woman needs her own income and a room of her own if she is to write fiction. Most writers would certainly prefer to have a dedicated space and regular pay. But Woolf was a privileged member of the intellectual upper middle class. Many writers – men and women alike – have had to make do with the kitchen table, the park bench or the crowded commuter train. Jane Austen wrote in the sitting room, hiding her pages when the creaking door warned her that someone was coming; Anthony Trollope worked on his novels during train journeys; James Joyce scribbled with a suitcase across his knees and his children playing nearby (although this may have contributed to the incomprehensibility of his prose to an extent that has so far been overlooked). Indeed, some of the most brilliant writers in the language have had day jobs they found tedious, tiresome or even hateful, but which have also influenced and inspired their work. What would Raymond Carver have found to write about if he had not spent the prime of his life doing mundane jobs that gave him an insight into the dark side of the American Dream? The life he railed against was the subject of his greatest stories. (And he was not the only one, as you will see when we discuss day jobs in Chapter 8.)

Which is to say: day jobs are perfectly normal. Most writers are also journalists, or teachers, or have an office job, or children. Most writers are too busy. They struggle with deadlines, wonder where their elusive muse has got to and worry that they will never manage to organise their thoughts. The author who sits serenely in his Mediterranean villa as he pens his latest masterwork is the exception, not the rule.

Writing careers as we now know them are part of the mercantile, capitalist system. Words are the stock-in-trade of writers, whether they are printed or performed, and writers sell these words for a fee. The law of copyright came into being to give authors the right to retain the ownership of their work beyond any agreed and specific sale. This model is changing, and anyone making an income out of writing now needs to be aware of the seismic changes that are revolutionising the publishing industry and the print media. I'll look at the Internet later – it's both a threat and an opportunity for authors. Fundamentally, though, it undermines the rights of authors over what they produce, and is the death knell of a system of copyright that had its beginnings in the sixteenth century. If that puts you off, go back and look at the Rilke quotation at the beginning of this chapter – you are in the wrong job. But I suspect that you already know the odds are stacked against you – and you are going to carry on anyway. And you are not alone, as you will see.

In the pages to come I will be looking at the various aspects of the life that you will lead as a working writer. This includes learning to develop your skills, networking, finding ways to get useful feedback, dealing with professionals, money, day jobs, publicity, writing online and how to cope with the inevitable pitfalls. I'll also look at the opportunities for established writers, and for those who want to make a social contribution. And there is a list of major competitions – winning a prize is a good way to get attention, as well as doing wonders for your self-belief.

Writing Careers: The Lowdown

- Getting a book published is not a happy ending: it's a new beginning.
- There is no route map from this point – you must find your own way.

- Publishing is a business, and books are products whether you like it or not.
- Few writers get rich; if money is your motivation try something else.
- Writers with day jobs are the rule, not the exception.
- Busyness can fuel creativity and most successful writers have too much to do.
- If you are a writer, you will write no matter what. This is your vocation.

CHAPTER TWO

The Words

'What one wants for writing is habit.'   Virginia Woolf

This is not a 'how-to-write' book, but of course writing must be at the centre of an author's life. So, while I am not advising you about what goes onto the page, in this chapter I will talk about the act of writing. What you need, as Virginia Woolf says, is 'habit'. Ideally, you should be writing something, anything, every day.

The issue of time, how you use it and whether you can be bothered to use it for writing, is closely linked to the issue of day jobs and the constraints that Life places upon Art. One of the reasons that many would-be writers give for their endless procrastination is that they just don't have the *time* to write a novel. But they do have time to go to the gym three times a week, and watch *EastEnders* and shop for vintage bargains on eBay. The truth is that most of us do accomplish the things that we really want to accomplish in life, as long as we make them a priority. Not writing is about not thinking it is important enough. No matter how busy you are, there is enough time if you really do want to find it. We can't all throw in the boring office job and live in a seedy Paris apartment pretending to be Samuel Beckett. But we can all find a few extra hours every week. Reading interviews with working writers makes it plain that busyness is part of the territory. These are not people who are waiting for the muse to strike: they are people who take every chance they have to get the words written.

Children's author Harriet Goodwin is one example. Her first book, *The Boy Who Fell Down Exit 43*, was published in 2009, became a Book of the Month in Borders and was shortlisted for a *Blue Peter* award. Her second book came out at the beginning of 2011. She also has four young children, and has continued to work as a professional mezzo soprano. (Before having children she had a successful full-time singing career and spent much of her time touring.)

'I don't think of myself as having a day job at all,' she says. 'Motherhood is the most important thing in my life, and I fit other things around it. When my first child was born I was still touring for a while, and I had to ask myself, Do I want to carry on with serious singing? And I realised that I couldn't go on with touring, which could mean being out of the country for weeks at a time.

'Writing came out of the blue: I had a dream one night about a boy who crashed through the surface of the earth into an underground world, and when I woke up I thought, This is a book! I wrote it little by little, sometimes only for ten minutes a day.'

The flexibility of writing is very different from the demands of working as a professional mezzo soprano, but Goodwin manages to do both by restricting her singing engagements to those in the UK and using her time as creatively as possible. 'I don't watch TV and I don't do any ironing!' she says. 'And there is a pattern to my days sometimes – when I was writing the second book I would write from nine till one, then go for a swim or a walk and then collect the children. I am pretty active. I also do a lot of school visits, which I really enjoy, though it is time-consuming. And I don't do much at weekends – that is family time.'

This may sound like a pressurised existence to some, but Goodwin loves every minute of it. 'The children are very proud of me, and they know I have time for them as well as writing. I am struck by how unbelievably lucky I am to have all these things in my life. I just do it, it's part of who I am.'

Finding Time and Space

Harriet Goodwin's story speaks for itself: if you really want to write, then you will find time and space to do it. When Ted Hughes lived in a small flat in London with Sylvia Plath, some of their friends were critical of the fact that she wrote at the table in the sitting room, while he wrote his poetry on a card table wedged into the cramped and windowless hallway. But he later said that this was one of the best writing spaces he ever had, and he worked there very happily and productively.

None of this is easy, however. You do need to ask yourself whether you are prepared to put up with the inconvenience, the frustration and the vast expense of time and energy that a writing career involves. The end point is always far ahead – and you may never reach it. Like me, you may find that even when you are published the fight for time and self-belief is not over, and that you still need to 'keep buggering on', in the words of Winston Churchill. I do know people who wanted to write one book, which they did, and they are happy. I know others who wanted to be published in some form, and they were, and that was it. And I know many, many others who are like me. They want to write no matter what. They need to write and nothing will stop them. And they *will* write, as long as they have the physical and mental capacity to do so. But, before spending years of your life tapping away at your laptop, do take time out to think about whether this is really what you want to do.

Why Do You Want to Write?

Most writers describe writing itself as a compulsion, an over-whelming urge to order and control experience or express their ideas – an addiction that they cannot break. Some say they dislike the process itself, but still feel worse if they don't do it. Although writing is a wonderful outlet for self-expression, this doesn't mean that each time you write you will feel you have said anything worth saying. You will stare bleakly at the lines of utter drivel you have scrawled or typed, and your head will feel as if it were gently caving in. Why do this when you could be going to the gym, or watching *EastEnders*, or following vintage items on eBay?

It's important to ask yourself what you want to write, and why. Do you have traumas to unravel? Scores to settle? Dreams that you have scribbled down each morning that you have strung together to make a fascinating experimental novel? Or perhaps some bedtime stories that you have told your children, which you think deserve a wider audience? While it is possible that, if you have penned any of the above, you could hit the publishing jackpot, it's extremely unlikely. You will have to move a very long way from these thoughts and jottings if you want to be taken seriously as a professional writer.

If you want to be a professional writer, you need to think like a professional, organise yourself like a professional and write like a professional. Nobody is interested in your ideas just because they are your ideas. If you want to get your work out there, you need to see your experiences as raw material and make them as appealing and relevant to other people as you can. If you don't like the sound of that, then don't even consider a writing career.

You must remember that there has never been a worse time to try to get a book deal. There is a huge global recession, business is bad in all sectors, not just publishing. But in publishing there is a 'perfect storm' because world recession and the rise of the Internet have coincided. There is no certainty that books will continue to be published and sold in the format that we know and love. Young people are reading less and less on paper and more and more online.

If this is the right career for you, then the process of writing should be satisfying in itself, even though it is time-consuming and often irksome. No one should write because the end (international celebrity) justifies the means (churning out words instead of having a life). If you do, then you are setting yourself up for terrible disappointment. Fame should never be the spur.

Getting Started

Once you have established that this is the only way to go, and that if you don't write you will go mad, then the next step is to make sure that you act on this decision. Just as the world is full of portly people who are always about to diet, it's also full of novelists-in-waiting who have stockpiled the leather-bound notebooks, but aren't quite ready to begin the actual writing. Not being quite ready is common among real writers as well as would-be ones, of course, so it's worth looking at what stops us from starting.

While time management is an issue for writers, and there are tactics you can use to get more writing done, it is important to recognise that procrastination is not just about being disorganised. Nor is it about laziness. Procrastination is caused by fear and misplaced perfectionism. We put things off because the unrealised project can always live in our imagination in a perfect form. There is no novel that is as great as the unwritten story inside the writer's head.

Even Flaubert, who some critics believe came pretty close to perfection at his best, shared this frustration. In his exquisitely written masterpiece *Madame Bovary* he wrote, 'Language is a cracked kettle on which we beat out tunes for bears to dance to, while all the time we long to move the stars to pity.'

Fear and the desire to write something brilliant are closely linked. The fear is that we will write something mundane, pointless, embarrassing. The blank page is often cited as a challenge to any writer – now we also have the empty screen to contend with. Working directly onto a computer can be even more daunting than writing on paper. As soon as we type them, the words look so finished, so professional, that it can make the ideas and sentences seem as if they should be equally finished and complete. A computer gives your work a sort of instant permanence, apparently too formalised to be tampered with. And yet, as Hemingway said, 'The first draft of anything is shit.' This applies just as much to your immaculate printout as it does to the indecipherable pages of a notebook. My advice is to scribble down ideas, draw mind maps, free-write, write in crazy capitals on blank paper. Anything to break out of the straitjacket of unrealistic expectation. If you lower your expect- ations of yourself, and just write, the urge to procrastinate will be reduced. See it as doodling or sketching, rather than producing a latter-day *Brothers Karamazov*.

This is not a 'how to write' book, and this is as near as I will come to giving you advice about the work itself. Here are my words of wisdom:

- Write every day.
- Set yourself a low target – one friend of mine aims at five minutes. Every day. She usually exceeds it.
- Take the pressure off. Write in odd places, at odd times. Don't enslave yourself to routine.
- Carry a notebook with you at all times, and try to catch lines of conversation, scenes, ideas, as you go about your daily business. This is the equivalent of an artist's sketchbook.
- Follow the example of Kate Long, author of *The Bad Mother's Handbook*, and keep a notebook by your bed.

If an idea strikes you at 3 a.m., write it down. You don't even have to switch the light on.
* Read voraciously, and don't stick to just one genre.

The Right to Write – and Keep Writing

Two very different writers that I'd recommend if you want to boost your motivation are Julia Cameron and Malcolm Gladwell. Julia Cameron's *The Right to Write* is a classic 'how to' book, and, although you may not find all her methods to your taste, she writes wonderfully about the rewards and joys of writing for its own sake. She is a champion of 'morning pages': keeping a notebook by your bed and writing before you do anything else each day. The idea is that you will be able to note down some of the half-asleep thoughts and dream-fragments that will float away as soon as you are fully conscious. I have managed to do this only rarely, but I developed my own equivalent of morning pages: a mad scrawl on the train to work. Almost invariably, I resist free-writing, assuring myself that I have nothing of any interest to say, that I am not in the mood etc., etc. Almost invariably I write down one or two things that really help me, either fragments of common sense and self-therapy, or ideas or scenes from whatever story I happen to be working on. Or new ideas. Or just random thoughts.

Malcolm Gladwell's *Outliers* is a call to action for anyone who likes to bang on about how much they love writing/want to be a published author, but doesn't quite get round to getting the words down. His theory is that all great artists have practised their art for a minimum of 10,000 hours. The public perception of genius is that gifted people are different from you and me, and, while he accepts that talent is unevenly distributed across the population, he points out that, without exception, those who excel are those who work the hardest.

Gladwell cites the work of the American neuroscientist Daniel Levitin, whose book *This is Your Brain on Music:*

Understanding a Human Obsession became an international best-seller. Levitin writes in Chapter 7:

> In study after study, of composers, basketball players, fiction writers, ice skaters, concert pianists, chess players, master criminals, and what have you, this number comes up again and again. Of course, this doesn't address why some people get more out of their practice sessions than others do. But no one has yet found a case in which true world class expertise was accomplished in less time. It seems that it takes the brain this long to assimilate all that it needs to know to achieve true mastery.

One example is the Beatles, who seemed like a bunch of effortlessly natural entertainers when they stormed Britain and the US in the early sixties. And their talent was of course beyond dispute. But the Fab Four weren't artless ingénues. Between 1960 and 1962, they made five trips to Hamburg, where they played seven days a week, often for eight hours at a stretch. Gladwell writes, 'All told, they performed for 270 nights in just over a year and a half. By the time they had their first burst of success . . . they had performed twelve hundred times.' Most bands, Gladwell points out, don't perform together that often in their entire careers.

You may not have the opportunity to immerse yourself in your craft in such a dramatic way, but you can make sure that you put in the hours. I've got children, and have always worked as a journalist or teacher to survive. I'm also pretty sociable and like a glass of red wine now and then. How did I find the time to write as much as I have? Like Harriet Goodwin I avoid TV and ironing. (Is there some sort of magic formula there?) And on a number of family holidays I've spent hours sitting in the sun scribbling at my novel, briefcase by my side. I started my current novel while spending a rather brisk week in Cornwall during which I sat on the beach at Polzeath, doing an annotated reading of

Macbeth with a towel over my head. I might sound like a pretty tedious holiday companion. But I reckon I have just about clocked up 10,000 hours.

The Long Haul

For most writers, developing a writing career is like climbing a mountain. Over and over, you seem to be about to scale the final summit, and over and over a new peak appears, higher up, further ahead. Getting published may seem like the final proof that you have achieved your goal, that you have been given a seal of approval as a real writer and a true professional. But this isn't necessarily the case. These days, it is not safe to assume that your career is established and that you are unassailable until you have published several novels, and are selling well. A slightly different template applies if you are a literary writer, in which case you might measure your success in awards and reviews. But for any writer, Nielsen BookScan rules, and publishing is a ruthless business.

(If you haven't heard of Nielsen BookScan, prepare to add this information to your armoury of knowledge about being a writer. Set up in 2001, it is a data provider that produces point-of-sale information on book sales to the publishing industry. Tracking of book sales used to be done without raw numbers. The *New York Times*, for instance, would survey hundreds of booksellers to estimate which books were selling the most copies, and publish rankings but not figures. Publishers tracked sales of their books, but tended to keep this information to themselves.)

And we have come a long way since Victorian times, when the readership for popular novels was so vast that publishers were scrabbling around to find enough writers to produce a sufficient number of new books to offer to the circulating libraries. No one is quite sure who 'readers' are going to be in the future, or what sort of fiction they will want to read, or what format they will choose to read it in, or whether they will be prepared to pay for it. Runaway best-sellers are still seen as the antidote to all of this, which means that either the very well-known or complete beginners are more likely to attract a publisher than a working writer with a track record. If you are a 'mid-list' author who is not (yet) a household name, you may well find that your publisher drops you in favour of someone it can market as fresh talent.

If that happens – and it has happened to me – it's hard. But the trick is to keep going. I was forced to realise that it was the writing itself that I enjoyed more than any other part of the publishing process, and spending more time – more of my 10,000 hours – pouring out more words and developing ideas. In a way it was a relief to be free of commissions and deadlines, and to be able to work on something just because I loved it and it inspired me. (Though at the same time I made a close study of the market, and became more savvy about what readers are looking for.)

Keeping going can seem like starting over again every day. It can seem like a mug's game. It can seem hopeless, ridiculous. You may even feel embarrassed about your own dedication to your Art. But take no notice of such feelings – carry on. Not because you will win the Man Booker, or make a million, but because this is one of the most rewarding ways that you can spend your time. And it's a terrible loss to turn away from your creative ideas just because they are not 'commercial'. In the following sections, I will be offering some practical suggestions about how to sustain yourself and boost your morale.

Keeping Company

A writer needs kindred spirits to keep going. That may mean other writers, but it also includes people who are on your team, who care about you and who are pleased for you when you succeed. I've found that, since being published, I have become more careful about whom I spend time with. This is not arrogant or ruthless: it is about survival. Those who aren't pleased for you, or who see your writing as a form of showing off or self-delusion, can stop you from working. It really is as simple as that. If you don't have much time, or much energy, put some distance between yourself and the friends and associates who make you doubt your ability. Writing circles can help, but so can good friends you can relax with, and fellow writers who know the score. This relates to the networking, which I deal with in Chapter 4. Knowing the 'right' people is not just about getting to hear about opportunities: it's about emotional wellbeing and support.

How to Boost Your Energy

As well as knowing people who are on your side and will root for you when the going gets tough, there are plenty of things that you can do to boost your energy levels and your self-belief. Julia Cameron advises her readers to take time out to recharge their creative batteries, and to get away from the written word some of the time. Go to a gallery, walk by the sea, take a trip to a city that interests you or a long country walk.

Going alone means that you are forced to reflect on what you are doing, and are more likely to be immersed in the experience – just as travelling alone can make your trip more intense and memorable.

Drugs and alcohol are not recommended as sources of inspiration for the professional author, in spite of the popular image of Hemingway et al., writing away with a glass of bourbon to hand. (In fact, Hemingway wrote five hundred words every morning, stone-cold sober, standing up.) Nicotine and caffeine are more use than booze – at least these are drugs that keep you awake. But exercise is more effective than any drug for sustaining energy and getting your brain working. The education consultant and motivational guru Tony Buzan recommends a twenty-minute burst of exercise every day. Jogging, swimming or walking will all do the trick – there is no need to start training for a marathon. Writers tend to be sedentary individuals, and fresh air and exercise might be fairly low on your list of priorities. But it really does work. I try to swim or go to the gym when I have a full day's writing to do, either first thing or at about three in the afternoon, when my energy flags. I never, ever want to go, and I have never, ever failed to feel better for it.

Ten Rules For Good Time Management

Rule 1: Keep a time log

If you can't work out how to fit writing into your busy schedule, then work out exactly how much time you are spending doing other things. For a week, make a note of everything you do, including sleeping, working, commuting, surfing the Web, watching TV, socialising, eating, shopping, household chores, taking exercise etc. Don't miss anything out – make detailed entries for one week. When you have done this, you should be able to get a picture of how you are using your time. And, unless you are exceptionally busy, there will be a gap somewhere, and you will be indulging in some sort of time-wasting activity, even if it's only looking at celebrities on the *Daily Mail* website. Shirley Conran, author of the 1970s best-seller *Superwoman*, believes that there are two ways of gaining extra time if all else fails – and she was advising working mothers with little wastage in their daily lives. You either get up an hour earlier each morning, or you go to bed an hour later at night.

Rule 2: Get an overview

Now, think about what you want to write, and what kind of timescale you are happy with. Do you want to write a novel before you are thirty? Or a screenplay by Christmas? Or six short stories in the next twelve months? Whatever your longer-term goal, break this down into smaller component parts. How much do you want to write in a month? A week? A day? My rule of thumb for a novel is two years – though Stephen King recommends writing the first draft of a novel in no more than three months. I found that writing around five hundred words a day was enough. This clocks up to 3,500 in a seven-day week, around 15,200 per calendar month and, therefore, more than 180,000 words in a year. You won't use all of those words, but you could chuck out around 90,000, and you will still have around 90,000 (give or take) left in your first draft. Five hundred words a day sounds like nothing. So little it's hardly worth bothering with. Easy to fit around just about any day job.

Rule 3: Draw up a schedule

It's not very Emily Brontë, but, once you know what you want to do, write out a schedule and stick to it. I write my word goals in my diary and also maintain a work schedule diary on my computer with my other novel business. Try not to let it slide, but, if you do, revise your schedule accordingly, either by setting a new deadline or (my preference) goading yourself on to produce a higher word count each day.

Rule 4: Be realistic

One of the great temptations of really getting down to writing is to expect too much of yourself. Don't set yourself targets that can't be sustained. Little and often is enough. Little and often is everything.

Rule 5: Just say no

Unfortunately, telling people that you can't do something because you are writing a book is seen either as a sign that you are utterly delusional, or as a wind-up. They'd be happy to go along to the pub quiz without you if you said you had to swot for an accountancy exam or mind the baby, but not if you say you are working on a novel. If you find it hard to refuse invitations for this reason, then tell a white lie.

Rule 6: Be consistent

Make your writing time a non-negotiable period of the day. Ideally, write when you feel fresh and mentally agile. Books have been written on commuter trains, but, if you are writing in these conditions, do schedule in some proper desk time, too, when you have peace and quiet.

Rule 7: Be single-minded

As well as saying no to social events, do not attempt to become a pillar of the community. Let others take on the mantle of parent governor, chairman of the local film society, volunteer tennis coach or whatever. Someone else can run the tombola stall. If you have a day job, a family, friends and some kind of domestic situation to sort out, then the time left over must be dedicated to writing, not making the world a better place. In any case, you can do that through your Art. Where would we be without literature?

Rule 8: Prioritise

Make a promise to yourself that you will give your writing precedence whenever possible. It's very, very easy to do everything else on your list, and let the writing – which gives you a sense of purpose and that there is a meaning to your life – fall off the edge. This is one reason why writing first thing in the morning can be a solution, even if you are not a morning person.

Rule 9: Delegate

If most of the domestic work falls to you, ask yourself why. Do you sincerely believe that stacking the dishwasher is your job? Or that parents are genetically conditioned to tidy their teenagers' bedrooms? Getting other family members to learn some self-maintenance skills is to do them a huge favour. If you live alone, see if you can cut more corners, and 'zone' your chores, doing the bulk of them in one go, and keeping daily jobs like cooking and washing up as simple as possible.

Rule 10: Don't forget to read

If your energy levels start to flag, don't forget that reading is part of a writer's job. Setting aside an hour or so at the end of each day to read a novel or nonfiction book is time well spent. If you can also read on your commute, that will fill your mental 'inbox' with thoughts and ideas. And the rhythms and patterns of other writers' prose will also enrich and inspire your own style.

Book doctors and writing coaches

You don't have to go it alone if your morale and self-belief are flagging. For a fee, you can use the help and advice of professionals. There are a number of reputable literary consultancies and individuals who will offer you well-informed advice about how publishable your work is, and what the industry is looking for. If they think your work is outstanding, they may even offer to help find you an agent from among their contacts. Major consultancies working in this field include the Writers' Workshop, a team of 70 authors and screenwriters; the Literary Consultancy, which was founded by a former editor from Virago; and the Cornerstones Literary Consultancy.

An organisation that takes a holistic approach is the Writing

Coach, set up by Jacqui Lofthouse, a graduate of the University of East Anglia Creative Writing MA programme. Her company works with authors and would-be authors from an early stage, offering advice about completion, focus and motivation as well running a consultancy service for writers with finished manuscripts.

Contact any of the above organisations, and you can see whether their services might help you. The established companies are not cheap, but they are respected in the publishing industry. If you can afford it, this can be very useful. Their feedback is not always flattering, but they will give you an insight into the professional editing process and make suggestions about the rewriting and/or editing that your book needs if you want to impress an agent or publisher.

There are numerous independents and smaller companies working in this field. Be sure that the firm or individual you hire is credible and has a proven track record. Personal recommendation is important. All the companies I have listed have endorsements on their websites and are well established. There are other operators in this field who will take a fee and offer little in return apart from a misleading critique.

Kate Long

Kate Long is the author of the best-selling novel The Bad Mother's Handbook, *published in 2000, which was made into a TV drama starring Catherine Tate. Since then she has published another four novels and a number of short stories.*

'I started writing in about 1994,' she says. 'I had been through a period of infertility treatment, miscarriages and such, and then I finally got pregnant. During the fertility treatment I found writing a real distraction. It gave me a feeling of being in control, which was completely different to waiting to see if the treatments were working. Happily my first son was born in 1997, and three years later, during the months after my second son arrived, I completed the first draft of *The Bad Mother's Handbook*.

'How did I do it? Because of the kids I had very little social life and so I filled up what spare minutes came my way with writing. Irritatingly, in an interview soon after the book came out, I made a daft, throwaway comment regarding time management which has followed me about ever since: I claimed that "I just wrote whenever there was nothing much on TV." I suppose I was trying to make the journalist laugh. But the truth is, while I was writing my first novel I didn't watch TV properly for about two years!

'You do need to be really organised. If you say that you are going to deliver a manuscript for a deadline, then you have to try very hard to make sure that happens. You pull out all the stops to keep that promise.

'And you also have to work hard. Weekends aside, I don't take many days off at all, and I'm at my computer for 9.15 each morning. My big fear is that if I stop I won't be able to start again. So I don't stop. I keep a pad of paper and a pen by the bed, and at night, in the pitch dark, I see the next chapter unfold and I scribble some ideas down. In the morning I go to the computer with my spidery notes and amazingly it is usually okay. In fact, I am often surprised by what I have written.

'Writing every day keeps the writing going; it makes the whole process much easier to sustain. But, if external/domestic events do overtake me and swallow up my work time, getting down one single sentence can be enough for me to maintain the momentum. I think novice writers who set themselves the task of writing a thousand words a day might sometimes be being too ambitious – what I would say is, write *what you can manage* and find your own natural word count. Essentially, just keep going, doing a little and often. Writing's a bit like dieting. It's the cumulative effect that counts.'

Time Management and Motivation: The Lowdown

- Take a step back and think about why you write, and what you want to write. Be sure that this is the life you want.
- Get the momentum going, and make sure that your writing life is happening now, today.
- Aim low, and set yourself deadlines and goals that are achievable. Make sure you achieve them.
- Recharge your batteries with reading, exercise, and other interests.
- Remember that excellence comes with practice, no matter how talented you are. Malcolm Gladwell recommends '10,000 hours'.
- Spend time with people who make you feel that you can do it, not the naysayers.

CHAPTER THREE

Learning Your Craft

'It's none of their business that you have to learn to write. Let them think you were born that way.'
Ernest Hemingway

Once upon a time, there were no creative-writing courses. Not even in America. And yet there was no shortage of writers. Dickens did not sign up to a local-life writing workshop when he began his career: he wrote journalism and 'sketches' and learned by trial and error. George Eliot had no qualifications at all: as a woman she wasn't allowed to study at university. Instead, she read prodigiously, familiarising herself with Greek and Roman mythology. Dostoyevsky studied Shakespeare, Pascal and Victor Hugo, and was a literary celebrity by the time he was twenty-four.

Anyone who writes a good book has learned a craft, as well as expressed themselves as an artist. We grow up with language: we hear it, speak it, read it, write it. As we develop as writers, we use language to express our own thoughts and experience, but as part of that process we draw on older sources, anecdotes, family myths, fairy stories and even nursery rhymes. Writing doesn't just come upon us, like speaking tongues. It's a learned process and one that is enriched by practice, and by reading – both our contemporaries and writers from earlier times. Jeanette Winterson says her love of the English language was nurtured by her upbringing as the adopted child of Pentecostalist parents: the King James Bible has been hard-wired into her imagination.

In that sense, creative-writing programmes are just formalising a process that has always been part of the writer's progress towards producing their own work. Equally, you don't have to win a coveted place on the creative-writing MA at the University of East Anglia to learn to be a better writer. Your local writing circle might do just as well, if it's a good one that emphasises that reading and writing are interdependent.

The role of such programmes and courses is not to teach students how to write in a narrow, prescriptive way, but to share ideas and practices that have worked for others, and that are likely to help students focus their efforts in an effective way. The best courses stress that writing itself is the core of any writer's life, and workshops and independent writing will be a continuous feature of the programme. As an 'early career' writer, you don't need to go on a course: you can just as easily teach yourself, and self-discipline is vital whether you are studying formally or not. However, writing courses aren't just about learning: they are also about forming useful networks, both with tutors and fellow students.

Finding a Course

But how do you decide if you need to go on a course, and choose the one that is right for you? There are two traps for the unwary here: assuming that all creative-writing programmes are a scam; and blithely signing up for the nearest course without researching the market. Spend at least as long looking as the options as you would if you were buying a new car or dishwasher. Even a few days at an Arvon centre (the Arvon Foundation runs residential creative-writing courses in four centres in the UK) will cost hundreds of pounds; most MAs will set you back at least £3,000, and this figure is likely to increase dramatically in coming years.

And don't underestimate the value of such courses. There is evidence that a degree course can lead to publishing success. Research carried out by *The Times* in January 2010 found that 'the popularity of such courses has infiltrated literary prize lists' and suggested that degree courses are increasingly 'the springboard to success'. *The Times* found that, of eighty-nine authors on the shortlists of the Man Booker, the Orange Prize for Fiction and the Costa Book awards in the previous five years, almost one in five had an MA in creative writing or an equivalent qualification, and two were teachers of creative writing. Over the same period, eight of the finalists for the Orange Prize for Fiction had a master's degree in creative writing.

Professor Gerard Woodward, a novelist, poet and senior creative-writing lecturer at Bath Spa University, believes that muddled thinking lies behind criticisms of writing courses. Writing in *The Author*, he comments,

> People who claim that creative writing can't be taught tend to be getting two things mixed up – the technical craft of writing on the one hand, and the emotional/creative impulse on the other. It is probably true that the latter cannot be taught, only encouraged, and students who have got as far as gaining a place on our MA course have probably got it already.
>
> The technical craft of writing, on the other hand, can be taught like any other skill. You could argue, of course, that students could learn all they need to know about writing from reading the works of great writers, figuring out how they did it, and then copying them. But that is a bit like telling someone to learn the violin by going to a concert hall and watching a great violinist playing their instrument. Except for the innately gifted few, mere observation isn't enough.

One additional point: as I have mentioned, this is not a book about 'how to write', but 'how to be a writer'. Being a writer means being a reader. If you can't afford to enrol on a writing degree course, you can still join your local library and read everything that relates to your writing – and preferably everything else as well. As a writer of fiction, you should be a voracious reader with a good knowledge of both the classics and contemporary fiction. If you are a nonfiction writer, you should be reading about your subject. This is partly because you need to know what your potential readers are reading now, so that you can engage them more effectively. But it's also because the written word is your stock-in-trade, and you need to be an expert in your field. You might be inspired by a picture, a memory or a song, but in the end it will always come back to the words. And, not least of all, reading is one of life's greatest pleasures. You can recharge your creative energy, become better informed about what you are doing, and lose yourself in another world. What more could you ask for?

Researching The Options

When it comes to finding the right course, doing your research is essential. Ask around, talk to anyone you know who writes either professionally or as a hobby, and get a good overview of what is available, both nationally and locally. *Mslexia*, the magazine for women who write (which is also useful for men), lists the following variants:

- WRITING GROUP: regular meetings in which members give feedback on each other's work. No tutor.
- WRITING WORKSHOP: regular tutor-led meetings at which new work is written and feedback is given by both the tutor and fellow students.
- DAY OR EVENING CLASS: weekly tutor-led workshops with (usually) no formal assessment.

- MENTORING MANUSCRIPT OR SERVICE: feedback and advice on an individual's work given by a single tutor.
- SHORT RESIDENTIAL COURSE OR WRITING HOLIDAY: intensive series of tutor-led workshops, plus some individual feedback sessions.
- DEGREE COURSE: university-based, tutor-led workshops plus lectures, with formal assessment.
- ONLINE OR DISTANCE LEARNING: all of the above options available in online and/or distance learning format.

Just as there is no shortcut to establishing a career as a writer, there is unfortunately no easy way of getting your head round all these various options. Subscribing to specialist journals like *Mslexia* and *Writing Magazine* can help, and there are numerous websites worth checking out. (*Writers' & Artists' Yearbook* is an invaluable resource for this – make sure you get hold of the latest edition.) But serendipity can play its part. Be practical about the amount of time you have at your disposal, and, if there is a writing group in a pub up the road or in your local community centre, give it a try. These groups and classes do not require a lifetime's commitment, and learning to give and receive feedback can take place in a free writing circle just as effectively as it does as part of a prestigious MA programme. Every single one of the options listed above has played a part in helping develop the talents of writers who are now household names or who have won literary prizes, so don't assume that you have to invest large sums of money in your training as a writer.

When deciding whether you want to study for a formal creative-writing qualification, there is one caveat (apart from the expense, that is). University creative-writing programmes have to prove their academic credibility. As a student, you will have to analyse your work in academic terms, and deconstruct the creative process in an intellectual way, which may seem unnecessary. When I studied for a creative-writing certificate at Sussex University in 2000, I was very unhappy about this. My children were young, and I felt guilty about time spent away from them. I had hired a nanny to bring them back from their nursery and babysit till my husband got home from work, so every second had to be accounted for. Writing essays about fiction seemed like a spurious activity, designed to placate the university authorities rather than to help me become a better writer.

Once I began studying for a doctorate in creative writing, I began to take a very different view. The creative process may be mysterious and unpredictable, but that doesn't mean that it can't be analysed. Looking at the way you write, assessing and considering your themes and inspirations, and reading and investigating the work of writers who have influenced you will add depth to your work, as well as enriching your imagination and fund of ideas. And it will also help you to write with a sophistication and self-awareness that will increase your chances of publication. Writing fiction cannot be neatly divided into different categories, and, far from forcing students to do this, a good degree course can help you to exploit your creative, intuitive 'right brain' more effectively.

You may not like everything about academe. I struggle with some of the specialist language myself. (What would George Orwell make of terms like 'praxis', 'trope' and 'narratology', I wonder?) But the goal is still worthwhile: increasing your understanding of your own imaginative process, and that of both your peers and the canon of published writers that already exists. The two processes – writing fiction and analysing the process of writing fiction – feed off each other.

How to Choose The Right Degree Programme

If you have decided to go down the higher-education route, how do you set about choosing an MA or degree programme? UCAS (Universities & Colleges Admissions Service) lists around eighty institutions that offer a creative-writing degree of some kind. It is time-consuming, but you need to research the available options, and see how each prospectus fits with your needs. Some are focused on the novel, others specialise in screenwriting or life writing. Some, like the Open University, offer online tuition. Others – like Birkbeck College in London – are specifically designed with the needs of working adults in mind. It's also important to look at the staff teaching on the course. All university departments should give you a full list of academics, their subject specialisms, research interests and publications, including their poetry collections, novels, plays and screenplays. (If a creative-writing tutor is not published at all, then alarm bells should ring. At the very least, ask yourself how good their industry contacts are likely to be.)

Bear in mind that this is still a very new area. The programmes that are run by these various institutions have been set up by academics and writers with a background in teaching English literature or fiction or poetry – they have brought their individual vision to the course and developed it accordingly. There is no centralised authority for creative-writing programmes in the UK, and no national benchmark for what a course should cover. One very useful source of information is the National Association for Writers in Education (NAWE), which has commissioned a number of students on creative-writing courses to write about their experience. This includes feedback from a number of mature students who have given up their jobs to study creative writing full time.

NAWE's website has a number of suggestions for prospective students. You could start with the following questions:

- Will you have time to work on your own creative writing?
- Does the course help you to develop your understanding of the writing arts generally, so you can improve your

understanding of the context in which you are working?
- Is the course a good fit with your personal strengths? For instance, do you thrive in writing workshops, or do you prefer to work one-to-one on your writing? Look for courses that offer the kind of teaching that you will enjoy.
- How is the course structured? One of the best approaches is to begin with an introduction to the basics, and end by completing a major writing project, with the support of your tutor.

But there are no hard-and-fast rules. Thousands of students study for first degrees and MAs in creative writing every year. This is a good starting point for a writing career, but studying a different discipline entirely might be a source of material, ideas or even a rewarding day job. Psychology has an obvious relevance to fiction writing, and there are well-known writers – such as Frances Fyfield, Jed Mercurio, Alexander McCall Smith and C. J. Sansom – who are from a legal or medical background. Scarlett Thomas, author of *The End of Mr Y* and *Our Tragic Universe*, is currently studying for an MSc in ethnobotany (the scientific study of the relationships that exist between people and plants).

If you are short of time or have family responsibilities, the Open University is a good place to study – virtually, of course. It runs a number of part-time fiction courses, one of which I have taught myself. OU courses are rigorous, well constructed and carefully monitored, and you will get useful feedback from both your fellow students and your tutor. But contact is almost exclusively online, which doesn't suit everyone. Most one-year courses run only two or three day schools, and students who want lots of face-to-face contact with other writers might find this disappointing.

Ultimately, courses are very useful – but you get out of them only what you put in. If you decide to go down this route, do it with clarity of purpose, determination and a positive attitude, and you will improve your writing and increase your professionalism. But don't expect a shortcut to publication, or a quick fix of any kind. And be prepared to give something back, to read the work of your fellow students with care and attention, and to help them improve the quality of their writing. The best creative-writing groups and courses are small communities, offering mutual support as well as considered criticism.

And don't be deceived by those who rubbish such courses – there is no shortage of talented students. Gerard Woodward of Bath Spa says he is overwhelmed by the sheer number of gifted writers he teaches.

'Perhaps a third of our forty or so students are producing work that could be published straightaway,' he says, 'and of the rest many will reach that standard over the next few years. The sad economics of publishing means that there simply isn't space in the nation's bookshops for another crop of Bath Spa novelists every year, so only a small proportion of our students will ever be published. The notion that an MA in creative writing automatically leads to a lucrative career as a published author is quickly shaken out of the few students who may be harbouring such a dream. Not wanting to sound too Darwinian about it, it will probably be the most determined and persistent as well as the most talented of our students who eventually make it.'

This is a theme I will be returning to. There are no fail-safe routes to a successful writing career, but a combination of talent, hard work, persistence and professionalism will set you in the right direction. And – unless you are very hermit-like indeed – my strong advice is to sign up for a writing course of some kind, whether it leads to an academic qualification or not.

Blake Morrison

Blake Morrison has been professor of creative writing at Goldsmiths College, University of London, since 2005. He is an established writer himself, with a background in literary journalism, as well as being a well-known poet, screenwriter and novelist.

'At Goldsmiths, you have a tutor and your peer group is a workshop of ten people,' he says. 'You gradually learn to pick out the people whose judgements mean something to you – and those whose judgements you are going to ignore. Many students form friendships that last long after the course is over. There is a sense of being in a little community, with other people who are trying to write. If you have always worked alone, you can now work in a serious way with others. You are less isolated.

'Students also learn to look at what they have written through the eyes of another person. Something that seems obvious to you is often not at all obvious to someone else. Being able to communicate with your readers is essential.

'We are all blind to our own faults, I think. Even very practised writers. And I don't think it gets any easier. Each time you start another book, it's like starting again. Maybe you do acquire certain skills along the way, but each new project has a different challenge – and throws up new obstacles.

'There is this gap now between the publishing world and the huge number of people coming off these many courses. I think we are realistic at Goldsmiths and that most of the people who come to us are realistic too. There may be one or two who are dazzled after seeing the Man Booker Prize on television, or reading a profile of Zadie Smith. But most of them are simply putting writing at the centre of their life, in a way that they have not done before, and that's immensely valuable, irrespective of whether they go on to publish.

'I usually tell students to take their time, treat each new piece as practice and development, and keep reading. In terms of whether such courses are worthwhile, yes, of course they are. It is well over a century since the first creative-writing course was set up and it is heading for forty years since Malcolm Bradbury set up the UEA [University of East Anglia] programme, so I think – get over it!

'Yes, some tutors, and some courses, are better than others. But there are definitely skills that can be acquired – whether you sign up for an MA, go on an Arvon course, study at an institute or just set up a workshop with friends. There is no need to be isolated. The time comes when you want professional feedback and that is what these courses are for.'

Residential courses

- The Arvon Foundation runs residential courses throughout the year at four centres in Devon, Inverness-shire, Shropshire and West Yorkshire – courses in all writing genres, led by well-known writers (see www.arvonfoundation.org).
- The Writers' Summer School is held each August at the Hayes Conference Centre, Swanwick, Derbyshire – the oldest established of the British writers' conferences, set up 1949 (see www.swanwickwritersschool.co.uk).
- The Writers' Holiday in Wales at Caerleon is a week-long conference that takes place in July – run for writers, by writers (see www.writersholiday.net).

Twelve universities with creative-writing programmes

- Bath Spa University (www.bathspa.ac.uk)
- Birkbeck College, University of London (www.bbk.ac.uk)
- Brunel University (www.brunel.ac.uk)
- University of Chichester (www.chiuni.ac.uk)
- City University, London (www.city.ac.uk)
- Goldsmiths, University of London (www.gold.ac.uk)
- Royal Holloway, University of London (www.rhul.ac.uk)
- University of Lancaster (www.lancs.ac.uk)
- University of Manchester (www.arts.manchester.ac.uk)
- University of Portsmouth (www.port.ac.uk)
- Sheffield Hallam University (www.prospectus.shu.ac.uk)
- University of East Anglia (www.uea.ac.uk)

Learning Your Craft: The Lowdown

- Anyone who writes a good book has learned a craft as well as created a work of art; good writing courses just speed up the process.
- Writing talent cannot be taught, but the craft of writing can be learned.
- There are a huge range of courses available now, so you must work out what you want and do your research.
- A degree or MA in creative writing is not a passport to publication: the odds are still stacked against you.
- Be realistic about the amount of time and money that you have – local workshops can be just as useful as MA programmes.
- Consider distance learning if you are busy and/or short of money. The Open University and the University of Lancaster run a number of creative-writing programmes.

CHAPTER FOUR

Networking

'I was commissioned to write my first novel, Sweet Desserts, *one night when I went over to a friend's house for dinner. The friend was Alexandra Pringle, then an editor at Virago Press, and now at Hamish Hamilton. I thought it was a joke at first, and laughed.'*

Lucy Ellman

Networking and publishing have bad names. One of the questions I am always asked at readings and author events is 'How did you get an agent?' and the tone is always suspicious, as if they're expecting me to say we both shared the same staircase at Oxford or Cambridge. And it's certainly true that relationships made at university – frequently at Oxbridge – can stand you in good stead if you want to be a writer. Sometimes it really is 'who you know' simply because there is not enough time to assess the relative merits of everyone you don't know. Equally important, there is immense value in networking with your fellow authors, who understand your pains and pleasures perfectly because they are sharing the same experiences.

And networking is indeed about who you know, who you like, who your friends are. It is not, repeat not, a conspiracy. Publishers are actually very keen on finding new voices. At the same time, mainstream publishers are risk-averse, and tend to want to repeat a tried and tested success, rather than experiment. The recession and the rise of the e-book have made them even more cautious.

This is not your cue to sit around the house in your jogging pants, complaining that your amazing talent will never be acknowledged because you just haven't got the contacts. Perhaps the only person you know in the world of publishing is the lady in the bookshop down the road, or the slightly helpful librarian who retired last year. If so, it is time to get dressed, get a good haircut and get out there.

Establishing Your Network

Publishing a book is a collaborative endeavour, you will need to work with a number of specialists and professionals if you want your book to become published, marketed, bought and read. But how do you find these people? Where are they? Start with your subject areas. What are you writing about? What are the relevant associations and interest groups in your field? And, no matter what your subject, you should join the Society of Authors, which holds regular networking events as well as running useful workshops about writing and publishing, and PEN, which hosts literary talks, fundraisers for writers overseas and other social gatherings. If you work in splendid isolation in your back bedroom, venturing out only to invest in the occasional packet of inspirational cigarettes, than you are less likely to get a publishing deal than someone who is always out and about at literary events.

You may think that is unfair. You may think that, if you are brilliant enough, all that should matter is your manuscript. You may think that if you send it out, and it hits the right person, on the right day, in the right mood, they will pick it up and read it and this will change your life. And you may be right. And perhaps you'll win a fortune on your Premium Bonds as well. However, if you take my advice, you will try to help your luck along a bit. The older I get, the less faith

I have in Destiny, and the more concerned I am with getting things done.

If there is a publisher who is just about to launch a new imprint, or a new editor who happens to be looking for exactly the kind of book you are just finishing, then it is extremely useful to be able to glean this information informally. You might read about it online or in the literary press, but it's likely to take longer. Developing some useful contacts is simply a matter of maximising your opportunity. In all walks of life, word of mouth is important, and the unofficial grapevine is the place to find out what is really going on. It is just as true in any large organisation or community as it is in the media. Gossip is not always idle – it can be highly productive. So it is no surprise that writers have to be networked too.

This is not about schmoozing, or working a room. (I have never seen that happen in real life.) It's about getting to know relevant people, and forming functional, friendly relationships with them. You don't have to be cynical about it – close friendships often develop from professional contacts. Just as we are statistically likely to form romantic relationships with colleagues – because they are there – we often find our most trusted friends at work. And you don't have to be loud and extrovert about it, either. Shy people can network. But it does take effort, and it will take a certain amount of time.

Networking with a Purpose

If you find networking challenging – which I must confess I do – then the solution is often to find some sort of shared activity, to network 'with a purpose', as they say in the business books. One way to approach this is to prepare a thirty-second 'commercial' or cocktail-party opener so that you aren't stuck for something to say. What are you writing about? Why? What inspires you? What are you reading? If you have written books/ short stories/poetry already, can you sum up the themes, and give someone a flavour of what you do? It's harder to do this than you might think.

Even an apparently unproductive evening may ultimately prove useful. I struggled along to one literary event in Brighton a few years ago. It was like being in a Posy Simmonds cartoon. The women were sporting Dame Hilda Bracket black and the men wore crumpled linen suits. The ceiling was low, the room was hot and sound seemed to swirl around me. I left early because I feared I would crush my wine glass when my hand went into muscular spasm.

My initial assumption was – obviously – that the whole thing had been a waste of time. A few days later, I found that an acquaintance who was there had given my email address to a Famous Writer who was organising a regular get-together for local authors. Out of that came the Brighton Moment, in which we read our work – in front of a sell-out audience – as part of the Brighton Festival. My piece was received far more enthusiastically than I could have hoped, and I found I actually liked performing. Through that I met some new writer friends, and made a lot of useful contacts, including Julie Burchill, one of the few people who was enthusiastic about my second book. I was at that first event for about an hour – so you might say that it was sixty minutes well spent. And I didn't even break the glass.

When my day job was freelance journalism, I wrote a number of articles about networking, and decided it was overhyped. To this day, I would never cold-call a 'useful person' and I still loathe walking into a room full of strangers. But I do know that there is no alternative to getting to know people in your field, and having some allies whom you can turn to for support and advice – and whom you can help in your turn. So pour yourself a large glass of Chardonnay, and get on with it. And do remember that, writers being the oddball characters that they are, most of them will feel just as awkward and ill-at-ease as you do. Authors are not natural air-kissers. Here are some pointers.

1. Join a writing group

Joining a writing group serves a dual purpose. It is a way of getting feedback on your work for free and developing your own critical awareness, and it is also a way of finding like-minded people who may know about competitions, festivals, literary events and other literary activities in your area. You may have to shop around until you find a group that suits you, and you may even have to set one up yourself. Public libraries sometimes host them, and you can also find out what is going on in your area through the National Association of Writers' Groups (www.nawg.co.uk).

Groups do change and develop over time, and getting together to discuss writing takes commitment and effort, but it is definitely worth it. I went to my first workshop in the early nineties at the City Lit in Covent Garden. This was a formal workshop, run by the tutor and playwright John Petherbridge, an inspirational creative-writing tutor. From that, I joined a small, women-only group that met fortnightly in north London. In Brighton, I was briefly a member of an all-male group of ranting pub poets, though we all felt that for various reasons I didn't quite fit in.

2. Go to writing conferences and festivals

Again, find out what is going on in your area. But be prepared to travel to events like Hay or Edinburgh – it will be worth it. If money is tight, economise by going along for one day if you live close enough, and save yourself the price of a hotel or B&B. Conferences are an excellent way of getting into conversation with fellow authors – there is always plenty to discuss, the speakers generally address issues that you are likely to have opinions about, and it's a painless way to learn more about the industry and what sort of writing is current, and to form new allegiances.

At festivals, don't just go and pay homage to the big-name

authors. Check out the fringe activities as well, and see who is running them. All sorts of interesting, entrepreneurial and creative types set up shop at these events, and you may come across someone running a literary magazine or website, or who is involved in digital publishing. Be open to possibilities – and ready to contribute to new or interesting ventures.

Get some cards printed – it's much more professional than scrabbling about for a biro and scrawling down your email address. And, if you do make a contact, follow this up with a quick hello as soon as possible afterwards. Ideally, send them some useful information about another event, a book you mentioned or with a suggestion that might help them in some way. Networking is about connecting to people and being helpful – networks thrive on partnerships.

On the other hand, don't forget to enjoy yourself, and don't beam in on people with a glint of desperation in your eye. If you relax, listen and absorb what is going on, you will meet other writers and relevant people without making a big deal of it.

Another big no-no is touting your manuscript around. People really *don't* want to read it, and, even if someone is kind enough to say they will, they will be speaking through gritted teeth. Leave your manuscript at home – there is plenty of time for that later on, when the contact is properly established. Even then, it is *quid pro quo*: every other writer wants their work read just as much as you do, so be prepared to read and comment as well as seeking feedback yourself.

3. Establish local links

Do this with bookshops, libraries, book groups and the local media. Thinking big is great – but most writers with any sort of profile started with their local town or area and built up from there. Almost certainly, there is more going on in your neighbourhood than you are aware of, and, once you start making contact with people, you will find this leads to other contacts. I will talk about the local scene again at the end of the book, but the key point is to make sure that you know what is going on in your immediate vicinity. You may be pleasantly surprised.

The first step is simply to make a list of the bookshops, publishers, social groups, libraries and local media in your area. Look up their details online, but also ask around and see if your friends know of groups or events that are connected with writing and the arts. Then, get in touch. Be systematic about this, and keep track of whom you have spoken to, making a record of their names and direct lines if that is relevant.

The next step is to go and meet people. If the group is an open-mic event or a writer's slot on hospital radio, then be prepared to share your work and join in. If your local bookshop runs author events, offer to speak or to help out if you aren't yet ready to present your own work. Not all of the local events will appeal to you – the secret is to find out what you really enjoy doing, and get involved if you can.

Think laterally: it could be that arts groups that are not overtly literary are full of people who love books, or who are networked with people who do write. So a film club or life-drawing class might be worth checking out as well as obviously bookish events. And don't forget networking events for free-lancers and the self-employed – these could be particularly useful if you decide to go it alone and bring out your book yourself. Remember – your back bedroom or home office is where you write. It is not where you sit and brood about writing.

4. Build up a list of industry and professional contacts

I used to be notoriously vague, but my background as a freelance journalist has helped me become more systematic. I now have a good contacts book, both conventional and virtual, and I know who I can go to if I need to. This has stood me in good stead in terms of both organising my book research and maintaining systems that are reasonably efficient. There is no need to be obsessive about it – just make sure you put names and details into your contacts book. (I would advise having a hard copy of contacts as well as a digital contacts file or a list of people in your phone – I have heard of too many disasters. But I am rather old-school in this respect.)

Admin, like losing weight, is best done gradually, and most effective when kept up on a consistent and regular basis. Binge admin equals migraine, but, if you must, you must. If you hate it, try to make your systems so simple that it is easier to keep them up to date than not to. For instance, buy a transparent folder and store all the business cards you are given there, in alphabetical order. To-do lists are also a good idea, particularly if you have a day job and keeping up with writing-related tasks is likely to be forgotten or sidelined. Try not to procrastinate when it comes to making That Call. There are people who gave me their contact details when John Major was prime minister who are still waiting to hear from me.

5. Use the Internet selectively

One of the great boons for the Shrinking Networker has to be the Internet. Facebook, LinkedIn, Twitter and Google are all useful in your networking trawl. You can find relevant people, join interest groups, become an expert in a new field and get in touch without fear of embarrassment. (Though I do worry if I email people and nothing comes back, and usually end up rereading the message I have sent, checking it out for gaucheness or stalker-eze. Email regret is an under-researched modern anxiety.)

6. Don't get sidetracked

Alarm bells should ring if your quest for contacts is turning into a displacement activity. People are vital to you, but so is your mental space and your imagination. Forget the world outside for as much of your day as possible.

There is more about the Internet in Chapter 12, but one point I would make at this stage is that it is a notorious waster of time. You need to *write* more than you need to do anything else, and my advice it set aside a limited period of time each day – or even every other day – to use the Internet in this way. I find it so distracting myself that, when I am in novel-writing mode, I leave the house and go and work in the local university library, without a laptop, and just write in longhand away from the electronic eye of the PC screen.

Celia Brayfield

Celia Brayfield is a novelist, journalist and cultural commentator. Her most recent novel is Wild Weekend *(Little, Brown/Time Warner Books). Her first three novels,* Pearls, The Prince *and* White Ice, *were international genre best-sellers.*

'I knew I wanted to be a writer when I was about nine, but for some reason I also knew I didn't want to write a novel when I was twenty – maybe because our English teacher gave us *The Young Visiters* to read and I was afraid of being laughed at. My father wouldn't allow me to go to university to read English, so I just read my way down the shelves at Brent public library: Tolstoy, Chekhov, Dostoyevsky, Stendhal, Balzac, Dumas, Maupassant – any writer I couldn't pronounce, basically.

'I decided to be a journalist and found my way into Fleet Street through *The Times* typing pool. And very *Mad Men* that was. But one editor after another realised I could write and I was a feature writer on national newspapers at a very young age. I wrote a daily column on TV for the [London] *Evening Standard* for eight years, and though it was mostly very mechanical it was wonderful training, because you had to deliver 750 words by 4.30 p.m. every day. Or you would be dead.

'I wanted to write the sort of books about women's lives that Colette or Mary McCarthy wrote – the English equivalent of [McCarthy's] *The Group*. I liked exotic settings – writing about life in a north London suburb would have bored me to death – but I also liked stories that were honest about women's lives and reflected the huge changes that women were going through at that time. Contraception that worked, feminism, the fact that it was just not possible to have the life your mother had. I was gathering material from my own life.

'I was a great listener. People liked me, they would tell

me things. As a journalist, I met so many brilliant, extra-ordinary people. And I was so lucky to be where I was at the time – I was determined to do the sixties properly, not by getting wasted but by making the most of what was happening. I made friends in fashion, music, publishing, the media, and I went to wonderful, wonderful events.

'I met my first agent through a friend of mine who was actually a food writer, and Carmen Callil, who later set up Virago, commissioned my first book *Glitter*.

'I'm not sure about the term "networking" but I do agree that it's important to know what is going on. And it is important to be part of a community of writers. Social relationships in life are essential and it is right and proper that you have social relationships with people you can work with, or might work with, or would like to work with. The creative economy is very well connected – groups, schools, movements. It's just something that happens naturally because writers know other writers.

'Just as every writer has a different way of working on a book, every writer has a different way of organising their career. For example, Amanda Craig has used social media very well, and made the most of this during the period while she is a mother in the thick of it. If you are a lad-lit writer, then going down the pub might be more appropriate.

'Social networking is amazingly useful for keeping up with publishing gossip. But the most important thing you can do is to write a good book. A really good book, a knock-their-socks-off good book. Nothing else that an author can do is any substitute for that. No matter how adept a user of Facebook you are, if you haven't written a brilliant book, it is no good.

'My advice is to do what works for you. You, the writer, are a work in progress. You have to keep feeding yourself, and you have to understand that that is what you are – a writer.'

Networking: The Lowdown

- It is true that 'who you know' counts if you want to get published – and stay published.
- But this does not amount to an elitist conspiracy – it is how all businesses and communities operate.
- Set out to establish mutually beneficial friendships and contacts in a systematic way.
- Use the Internet to search for like-minded writers and relevant interest groups, and also investigate the local scene.
- Don't worry if you are shy or introverted – schmoozing is not essential.
- And remember to enjoy this process – it is all about forging links with people who are congenial and who share your interests.

CHAPTER FIVE

The Professionals

'I think I am starving for publication: I love to get published; it maddens me not to get published. I feel at times like getting every publisher in the world by the scruff of the neck, forcing his jaws open, and cramming the Mss down his throat – "God-damn you, here it is – I will and must be published."'
Tom Wolfe

When you have worked hard enough on your novel, written and rewritten it, done the workshops and listened to the feedback, you may feel ready to send it off. But to whom? In the current market, it is advisable to use an agent. Many publishers won't even read an unsolicited manuscript if it's not submitted by an agent they know and respect. This chapter will look at the professionals who are essential to your career as a published author – the way that they work, their relation to each other (many agents have been publishers and vice versa) and what they want from you. This is important. Most books about writing give the impression that getting an agent will inevitably lead to getting a book deal, and that this will usher in a lasting period of success and happiness. For some authors, this has been the case. They are the lucky ones. For the majority, life continues to be complex and challenging. At the time of writing, there is enormous upheaval both in the publishing world itself and in the economy as a whole, and I am guessing that, when you read this, things won't have calmed down.

The bad news here is that the economic downturn and the uncertain future of the printed book have seriously undermined confidence in the publishing industry. Agents and editors are likely to say no to an unknown writer – not because they bear such writers any ill will, but because they are too busy already. They already have a long client list, consisting of authors with a proven track record. Some of these writers are famous and much in demand, and looking after them takes a great deal of time. Others may be having a quiet patch, or even having difficulty finding a publisher at all. None of this is easy for an agent. And backing a newcomer is a costly and risky business. Your manuscript represents another gamble, another shot in the dark.

What can you do? Be well informed. Know what the pressures are on them, as well as what the stresses are on you. And don't whinge. You'll just bore everyone, including yourself. Being well informed means making sure you know who's who, and how the publishing process works. It's not rocket science, it really is quite easy to understand. There are some people in publishing – not all – who like to maintain a certain air of mystery, as the British Royal Family used to before the onset of Diana and Fergie. This is because (a) it's more fun to work in a world that is seen as complex and arcane and (b) authors can easily get out of control. (Yes, it's sad but true. There are those who have gone before you who have given authors a bad name.) Before looking at the professionals you will come into contact with, let's look at the authorial place in the hierarchy, and start with a cautionary stereotype. (Bear in mind that I am using an extreme example here – and, if you follow the advice in the rest of the chapter, you can be sure that you won't make any of these mistakes!)

The Difficult Author

No writer sets out to be a difficult. But we are an intense breed, with a tendency to brood about real or imaginary put-downs, and we react badly to the success of colleagues. The transition from sensitive but socially functional writer to Difficult Author is an easy one to make. Alarm bells should ring if you find yourself shooting off aggressive but brilliantly worded emails; if you are too grand to use a mobile; if you won't tolerate any changes to your manuscript; and if you start hyperventilating because the proposed book jacket is the wrong colour. But the Difficult Author may also be a practised panicker, calling the publisher weeks before their book is due to come out, asking if it is too late to make a few small changes to Chapter Three. Or they may drink, causing mayhem in Orso's or similarly august establishments. (This style of authoring went out with Kingsley Amis; the cool thing now is one glass of white wine or, better still, stick to water.)

Remember that this should be a mutually rewarding, symbiotic relationship: your publisher needs good writers like you, and you need your publisher. Cordial relationships can lead to close working alliances – some writers have been with the same publishing house for decades, in spite of the uncertain times we live in. This won't happen to you if you have annoyed everyone you have come into contact with. The publishing industry is about relationships as well as books, and, if even if your sales aren't huge, your publisher is more likely to take on a second book if you are a pleasure to do business with than if you play the prima donna all the time.

Be warned: publishers do put up with Difficult Authors who are already famous, even if they don't like them very much. Their unspeakable antics take on the mythic status of tales from the battlefield. Do not take these people as your role models. Authors who are not already famous must behave themselves. Try to take on the persona of an attractive but biddable librarian from the Home Counties.

The Agent

A literary agent represents writers to publishers, dealing with the sale and negotiating on the writer's behalf. You will pay a fixed percentage (10–20 per cent; 15 per cent is usual) of the proceeds of the sale. Increasingly, a good agent is likely to advise you about the content and quality of your work, and make editorial suggestions. This is useful, because in a highly competitive publishing market it means that your manuscript will be in the best possible shape when it lands in front of an editor.

I would advise anyone who wants to put their writing career on a professional footing to get an agent. Don't just plump for the first person who offers to represent you, even though this is very tempting. If you are lucky enough to have a choice, make the most of it. This is one of the most important relationships of your publishing career, and is likely to last longer than your relationship with your editor. A good agent will have an extensive network and know which publishers are most likely to take your work. Beyond this, literary agencies vary hugely in terms of both size and their approach. Some are small, one-person operations, others are large firms with specialists in film, TV and foreign rights, and hundreds of clients. There are more than 170 UK agencies listed in *Writers' & Artists' Yearbook* – you need to do your homework and find out which agents might be the best 'fit' for you.

The agent's role

Do be realistic about what agents can do. They are typically intelligent people with publishing experience who have a passion for books and writing, but they have to be hard-headed to make their business work. Agents are the go-betweens linking authors – a weird and unpredictable group of people, as we have established – and publishing houses. Many of these are now huge global operations, with relentlessly commercial priorities.

It is not reasonable to expect an agency to nurture your work or to spend a lot of time telling you what to do with your unfinished book. That is not to say that this never happens – many agents work far beyond their paid working hours simply because they do love books. I've had generous advice from several agents in the last twenty years or so, for which I am extremely grateful. But this is not their job: if an agent does offer you feedback of this kind, it's because they think ultimately your book could be profitable. Take the advice, and get back to work.

If you want to know more about dealing with an agent in the early stage of your career, read *From Pitch to Publication* by literary agent Carole Blake, or Harry Bingham's *The Writers' & Artists' Yearbook Guide to Getting Published*. (See the resources list at the end of the book for more information.)

Remember, agents are busy. They are businesspeople. They don't like timewasters, lunatics, monomaniacs or sociopaths. They don't want manuscripts in fancy boxes, written in gold ink or attached to helium balloons. Yours is not the most brilliant script they have ever been sent. It will not change their life, and it will not make them rich. Do not put any of these suggestions into your submission letter.

If you want to be taken seriously by an agent, do the following:

- Research the market. Know the different categories used to classify fiction and where your book fits in. Show the agent that you are approaching your writing as a professional.
- Do your homework on each agency. Make sure they represent similar work to your own. Follow their submission guidelines. Most will want a covering letter,

a synopsis and the first fifty pages of your book. But
this does vary.
- Send your work to a specific agent and address it to
  them. Say why you have chosen to submit to them.
- Write a polished, professional query letter that is free
  of grammatical errors and spelling mistakes.
- Mention any referrals, personal connections or contacts.
- Keep sending your work out. Rejection is an inevitable
  part of the business.
- Let the agent know if this is a multi-submission, or if
  you are sending it exclusively to them. Don't fudge
  this – you may live to regret it.

The Editor

The commissioning editor is an important person in the
publishing process, and potentially a very important person
in your life. They buy or 'acquire' books, and are increasingly
sales-focused – some even come from a sales background.
Your book needs their unstinting support and your career
will flounder if your book doesn't get it. The commissioning
editor will work on your book in big-picture terms, carrying
out a 'structural edit' soon after you have delivered it. This
will look at issues such as the plot, characterisation and treatment of the main themes if it's a novel, and its coherence,
authority and accuracy if it is a work of nonfiction. They will
also look at your work in terms of style and its potential
appeal to readers.

Later in the process, when the major editorial changes
have been made, you will also work with a copy editor. Copy
editors are often freelance, and their role is to ensure that
your writing is consistent and grammatical. However, the
fact that a copy editor is less involved in the decision about
whether to continue publishing your work doesn't make
their role less important to you, the author. Their professionalism and eye for inconsistency is essential. If you have

a dynamic commissioning editor who loves your book, and a committed copy editor with a passion for the English language in all its finicking detail, then you have struck gold. But don't be too dependent on the editors you meet: in the course of your career you are likely to work with a number of different editors. Listen to what they have to say, and be prepared to learn from their expertise.

The Designer

The design team, as you would expect, will deal with the visual aspects of your novel. Essentially, the designer is responsible for the cover. And the cover has a vital part to play when it comes to selling your book. In a large publishing house, the design team will be designing hundreds of covers each year. Although the designer working on your title may not have read the whole book, he or she will have been briefed by the commissioning editor, who will collaborate with them throughout the design process.

As in other aspects of the publishing process, arm yourself with good information, look at the market more generally and don't allow yourself to have a knee-jerk reaction. If you don't like the design for your book cover, bear the following points in mind:

- No one else is as close to your book as you are; the mental picture you have built up while writing it is yours alone. There is no jacket in the world that will reflect that.
- A picture might paint a thousands words, but an image will have a hard job representing your 80,000. Be open to what the image conveys; don't expect miracles.
- Jackets are designed to look like other jackets, with a twist. At the time of writing, the jackets-du-jour show either the back view of a man in the middle distance, wearing something black, or the back view of a woman

in the middle distance, wearing something red. Your book will be in the shops, possibly even Tesco if you are lucky, and it will need an identifiable 'brand'. (You ask how this is possible, if all book jackets look the same? This is where the twist comes in.)

- If you really, really hate it, work out why. Be specific, and have specific suggestions for an alternative. (It may not be politic to point to the fantastic work done by another publishing house.) If you want to point to a positive example, find something this design team has done for someone else.

The Sales Team

Writers often shrink from the idea of 'sales' as if there is something rather vulgar about commerce. If this sounds like you, then think again. We live in a capitalist society, and your book is a consumer product as well as an artistic creation. And, if this bit of the process doesn't succeed, you will be spending more time on the day job.

It's the job of the sales team to sell your book to bookshops and bookshop chains in the UK and Ireland. The reps will visit the bookshops in their particular area, and will try to meet the sales targets they have been given. They will sell a certain number of books before publication, which is known as the subscription sale, or 'sub'. They target chains, independents, supermarkets and other retailers, and also sell to the Internet. They have a challenging job, and will start preparing sales material well ahead of the publication date – sometimes as much as a year. Overseas or export sales are even more challenging, and more complex.

The Marketing Department

The marketing team produces the material that is used by the sales team, and thinks through the strategy that they will follow. You may feel that this is of less interest to you than the role of the publicist (see below), but this is a very creative and competitive area, and a good idea from the marketing team could make all the difference to the sales of your book – more than an exciting interview in the *Guardian*.

The Publicist

While the marketing department is looking for ways of advertising your book – all of which cost money – the publicity team is looking for free publicity by using the media. Publicity also covers signings, festivals and readings – any event at which you might appear to promote your book and, indirectly, yourself. (I know it's embarrassing, but this has to be faced.) A good publicity campaign will take into account the subject of the book (easier with nonfiction than fiction), the author's personality, available slots at literary festivals and media opportunities. Again, this takes imagination, creativity and flair. If you think your book should have more publicity than it's getting, come up with some concrete suggestions and look at ways of contributing to the success of the strategy. Publicists are open to suggestions from authors and enjoy working with writers who have good ideas. (For more about this, turn to Chapter 11, which is about being your own PR.)

The Author

So what part do you play in all this? As a starting point, we will look at something that may seem very simple, even enjoyable, but that can be a make-or-break moment in your career. In my own case, a break moment, on more than one occasion. It is the art of having lunch.

Of course, you should know how to do this. You have a sandwich every day, and get bits of Cheddar cheese wedged in your keyboard. And you can speak, and drink from a glass, and operate a napkin. Presumably you have also eaten with other humans in the past as well, and know that it's necessary to stop speaking so you can chew occasionally, and that certain foodstuffs droop and dangle, while others stick to your teeth. But trust me, all these bodily memories will desert you when you're confronted with your new agent/editor/editor's fragrant boss. My current modus operandi if I am faced with a literary lunch is to eat almost nothing – a slice of seared tuna, maybe. And I drink water, keeping my hand rock steady. It was not always thus.

I have had two disastrous lunches in my career and would probably be living in Monte Carlo by now if I had conducted myself with more decorum. The first was in the eighties. I had mysteriously been shortlisted for a writing competition run by *Cosmopolitan* magazine. I was horribly shy in those days, really psychotically, weirdly shy. So shy that I couldn't walk out of my boss's office without my knees becoming inverts of themselves. The solution to this unfortunate problem was, of course, alcohol. Therefore, I was pleased to see, on my arrival at the Soho eatery where the award ceremony was taking place, that there was lots of it on display, and plenty of attentive waiting persons wearing black aprons pouring it out. Two glasses would just about see me right I thought, looking at the scary magazine girls in their important earrings. So I had two, and then my glass was filled up again, and I could see Jill Tweedie in the corner and really wanted to tell her how much I loved her writing, but apparently was still too shy. So I had another one. Then the list of prizewinners was read out backwards – or was it sideways? – and it turned out I had won.

It all goes a bit muzzy after that. There was Robert Elms talking about Sade and how it is lonely in a limo, and I said something really hilarious about limos not being lonely enough. No one laughed. Then I said some more stuff, segueing from Sade to comprehensive education. I ended up slumped on a chair, shouting about my painful transition – at the age of fourteen – from grammar school speccy to comp kid. When I looked up, it was still light outside and the room seemed to be a lot emptier. Jill Tweedie and Robert Elms had disappeared. Suddenly, we were back in the magazine office, and I was (apparently) sitting with the editor, pitching some feature ideas that I had scribbled down on the back of an Indian takeaway menu the night before. She was the sort of woman who kept her face very, very still.

I did get one feature in the magazine, a very short piece about Band Aid, which was big at the time. And that was it. The doors of Magazine Land glided shut, and I was left outside, with the nauseous certainty that I had not maximised my opportunity. Rule Number One: when you are dealing with professionals, *behave* like a professional. If you are shy, shut up.

My second lunch, much more recently, featured not drunkenness but a bad case of PLT (Publishing Lunch Tourette's). In my defence, I was dining with my delightful but gratuitously Sloaney editor, who made me feel like Nora Batty of *Last of the Summer Wine* fame, and her senior colleague, possibly one of the most elegant women in British publishing. I was wearing some Primark flares and a gypsy top from Oxfam. One sip of wine was enough for me now, a mum-of-two up from the sticks. I was laying down the law about everything. At one point, I said proudly. 'I'm not at all well connected, you know.' (*Why?*) And then I started showing off about how well read I was (I'm not, particularly) and correcting them about who wrote what in the 1930s.

I think, looking back, that I had decided that becoming a published author had somehow levelled the playing field, that I was now a Very Important Person who could hold forth about how utterly ordinary I was, not one of your Metropolitan types, thank you very much, while at the same time stressing that I was really terribly intelligent, thus settling any old didn't-go-to-Oxbridge scores that may have been niggling in the background.

This time the miasma was more gradual, creeping over

me like a sea mist as I travelled home on the stopping train to Brighton. What had I learned about the publishing house during our meeting? Nothing. What did I know about their list, the sort of writing that was selling, the kind of books they wanted to publish? Zilch. What did they know about me? That I got squiffy on one glass of champagne, was pretentious and tactless and knew no one who could help me sell my book. Opportunity had eluded me again. I was an Official Flake. Rule Number Two. You are *not* a Very Important Person (not yet, anyway). So make it your business to be useful. Or, failing that, polite.

A useful rule of thumb is to do pretty much the opposite of what I did on these two occasions. Once upon a time, the publishing lunch was a long, bibulous affair, and business might be discussed among a host of other subjects. Such lunches still happen, but they are not the norm. Nowadays, if your publisher is taking you out, they want to get to know you better, hear about your ideas for future books and see if they can 'do business with you'. Once you get to know them, and once you are an established writer, these lunches might be more relaxed. But essentially this is an informal business meeting. Do remember that you need to find out about them, just as they need to find out about you. The publishing industry changes quickly, trends in writing come and go, well-informed 'gossip' can be a source of useful information.

Don't be too nervous to ask questions that might seem obvious. Don't be too distracted by the excitement of being in an actual restaurant with actual publishers to keep your wits about you, and really listen to what your editor is saying. It may even be worth having a checklist of items that you want to discuss. And it is also worth preparing yourself by dressing the part and making sure you look well turned out and presentable. This doesn't mean you can't enjoy yourself – these occasions are often very pleasant – but remember why you are there. You are not there to get drunk, show off, talk nonsense or be rude. You are there to find out more about this mysterious but fascinating world, and to present yourself in the best possible light. And – ideally – to show that you are as delightful to meet as you are to read.

Publishing in Perspective

Getting a book published should always be a high note in an author's career. But, as we have seen, this is a protracted, complicated process that involves not only your agent and editor, but also the copy editor, designer, publicist and marketing department. The more you know before embarking on this journey, the better. Authors need to be clear what is involved and learn as much as possible about the role of each person involved. You also need to have reasonable expectations, and to understand that your book is one of many that their publisher is bringing out, and that most people working in publishing are overworked and underpaid.

At the same time, don't be grateful. Pleased, yes, but never grateful. The publishers aren't paying for your book because they are nice or because they like you (though they may well be perfectly charming people who love working with you). This is Business. And, if the B-word makes you think of Alan Sugar barking 'You're fired!' at some sharp-suited ambition zombie, then think again. Doing business simply means being paid for what you do. And the publisher is the paymaster in this case.

Remember that this is a two-way street. You may be thrilled, overwhelmed and even intimidated by this important breakthrough, but you need to take a deep breath and keep track of what is going on. What the publisher wants from you is professionalism. Think about your book as a tactile object, which it will soon become. Try to be clear about what it will take to make this book successful, and what you can do to make this happen. In return, what you want from them is a fair deal, and an understanding that buying your book means not only publishing it, but also putting enough marketing and publicity behind it to ensure that it has a reasonable chance of getting onto the public radar. At the same time, don't expect to be made a star overnight. This is not *The X Factor*. According to Nielsen BookScan, in 2011 the biggest sellers since records began in 1998 were Dan Brown and J. K. Rowling, followed by Stephanie Meyer and Alice Sebold. You may be a fan of one or all of these writers, but the book you have written may be far more subtle, niche, and small-scale. It is also a book by a writer whom no one has heard of, which has come out amid a sea of other books, by other writers. Some will be as obscure as you are. Others will already be famous as writers, or in other fields.

Dealing With Professionals: The Lowdown

Do:

- keep a sense of perspective and objectivity;
- find out as much as you can about the publishing process;
- think about the different roles of the professionals you meet;
- look smart, stay sober and behave yourself;
- make exquisite politeness your watchword;
- treat publication more like a job, and less like personal endorsement.

Don't:

- go mad, in any sense of the word, unless this is the unique selling point (USP) of your book;
- passively wait for publication to happen around you;
- be arrogant about your indispensable position as author;
- wear rubbish clothes, get smashed or show off;
- waffle on about yourself and share your random thoughts.

CHAPTER SIX

The Book Deal

'Almost anyone can be an author; the business is to collect money and fame from this state of being.' A. A. Milne

In this chapter I will set out each aspect of a typical publishing deal, and the part that the writer plays in this. I won't be giving advice about how much money to ask for, or specific suggestions about how to negotiate the best contract; this will depend on your situation. If you do have an agent, they will do the negotiating for you. The current climate is so unpredictable that advances have shrunk horrendously in recent years, and publishers are being extremely cautious. But, then again, you might be lucky. And the specific details of any contract will vary from writer to writer, and depend on the specific nature of your book as well as the size of the publishing house and the resources they have at their disposal.

Getting the Book Deal

Once your agent has read your book, suggested changes and is happy that this is a viable and attractive proposition for the right publisher, they will send it out to one or more editors. Most agents have particularly good contacts with a number of editors, and will know exactly what they are looking for, what kind of writing appeals to them and what sorts of books they have published recently. Your agent will make a decision about how to proceed to give you the best shot of finding a publisher and getting a good advance. One option is to call one editor and offer them the exclusive chance to see the manuscript before any of their competitors do. Another is to initiate an auction by sending the manuscript out to several editors at once.

The agent will decide on the best approach by taking into account the nature of your book, the current market and the editors they have in mind. You can discuss this with them, though, if you're a new writer, it is likely the names in question won't mean much to you. Unless you are very experienced and know the industry very well indeed, my advice is to let your agent make what seems to them to be the most sensible decision. You may love the idea of an auction, and imagine that a huge advance is the inevitable outcome. It isn't. Get this wrong and you may find that an editor who may have bought your book will be put off by the fact that it has already been seen and rejected by other publishing houses. So calm down and try to think about something else. Your agent knows far more about this than you do.

If one of the publishers in the frame likes the material, they will make you an offer, outlining their terms. These will include the amount of money they are paying as the advance and how this will be paid; the royalty rates; the territories in which the publisher will have the right to sell the book; and any subsidiary rights, such as translation and serial. Once these terms have been agreed and the publisher's offer has been accepted, the publisher will send you a draft contract.

The contract

Be sure that, when you see the draft contract with the publisher, you read it attentively and carefully. At this point, you may find there are points that you don't understand, or want to add some new clause that you feel will give your book a better chance. For instance, some writers ask for a particular PR company to be brought in to give the publicity for their book additional momentum. Don't be afraid to ask if you have any questions, or to make suggestions that you think will be useful.

Look in particular at the way that you will be paid. Typically, you will receive a third of the advance 'on signature' (i.e. when you sign the contract), a third when you deliver the manuscript ('on delivery') and a third on publication. If you are getting a large advance, this is particularly useful, as it spreads your tax liability over two or three years. But if you are getting only a small advance, it means that you are being paid an even tinier amount to do the actual work on your book.

In particular, make sure that you understand the legality of the contract, what the implications are in law and how this relates to your work as the author. Always ask your agent if you are unsure about something. If you don't have an agent, the Writers' Guild, which represents authors as well as screenwriters and dramatists, will read contracts for members to make sure they are legal and have no irregularities.

Here are some questions to ask about your contract:

- What does this contract require me to do?
- What does it require my publisher to do?
- What happens if my next book is late? How binding is the delivery date?
- Is there any chance, on the basis of this contract, that the publisher might decide not to bring out my book?
- Are they contractually obliged to publicise and market my book, and how is this worded in the contract?
- Is there anything unusual about this contract? Is this a 'standard' contract?

- How will I be paid?
- What are the arrangements about foreign and other rights?
- Can I buy back copyright to this book, and in what circumstances?

Whatever you do, one thing is not negotiable during this negotiating period:

- you *must* read your contract;
- do *not* sign anything you haven't read, or that you do not understand.

The Myth of the Mega-Advance

Do not enter negotiations for your new book expecting it to make you rich. You will be disappointed, and frankly, you will look foolish, too. It's tempting to fantasise about getting some mega-advance that will transform your life. All writers are susceptible to this. As the author of this guide I should know better, but I too have scanned the million-pound-property pages and mused about the comparative delights of a Georgian pile on the Brighton seafront and a castle in the west of Ireland. It is human nature to be greedy, unrealistic and easily distracted. And the careers of J. K. Rowling, Dan Brown, Stephanie Meyer and their ilk have entered the realm of folklore.

Time for a reality check. Advances for literary-fiction debuts plummeted in the three years up to when this book was published in 2011. According to *The Bookseller*, writers were being offered as little as £500. Payments of £1,000 or £3,000 are increasingly common – though, if you are writing genre fiction, the rewards are still likely to be more generous, with six-figure sums for a two-book deal still being reported. Remember that, even with such an apparently generous deal, this amount would break down to £50,000 per book, of which your agent is likely to charge you 15 per cent commission, or £7,500, and you will then pay 20 per cent tax on the remaining £42,500. Which leaves you with just £34,000 to splash out on that yacht you had your eye on. But it might take two years to produce each book, so that would mean earning half that sum. So you would end up with a net income of £17,000 for a year's work.

Well-known agents like Andrew Wylie may have made their name brokering huge deals for household names like Martin Amis. But even they say that the market is now split between high-earning authors, who command £100,000-plus for each book, and the rest of us, who are getting advances well under £10,000.

Foreign Rights

In the light of this, foreign rights are increasingly important. Though a book that hasn't caused even a ripple of interest in the UK is less likely to attract a foreign publisher, there is still a chance that, if your story could resonate with readers in another country, you might make a sale there. You might find that subsequent novels are published in another country – such as the Netherlands – even if you don't find a British publisher. Foreign publishers don't necessarily require a book to be published by a UK publisher once they have discovered an author and know they are popular in their own territory.

And, on an optimistic note, some overseas markets are expanding, and taking an interest in acquiring books by UK authors. India is becoming a major rights buyer, and so are China, Indonesia, Korea and Thailand. There is also more interest from countries in Eastern Europe and the Baltic States. A small story set in Tunbridge Wells may not be what they are looking for, but, if you are writing genre or literary fiction on a bigger canvas, you might find such deals are a useful additional source of income.

Some publishers are keen to pay a flat fee for 'all rights'.

If this is the case, and your book does have the potential to go global, make sure you understand how this will work. Any revenue earned from foreign rights is split between the publisher and the author (usually in the author's favour), so signing away foreign rights to a publisher doesn't automatically mean a loss of earnings. Take time to think this through: remember, you are a professional.

The Agent's Percentage

Your agent will negotiate on your behalf, act as your eyes and ears in the industry and deal with the nitty-gritty of contracts and daily admin. The more successful you are, the more useful it is to have someone who can shield you from constant queries and requests. ('I wish!' you may say, but you never know.) Being on the website of an agency also showcases your books and career to date, and anyone who wants to find out more about you or contact you is likely to do an Internet search for your agent.

The going rate for a British literary agent is 15 per cent for a UK book deal and 20 per cent for foreign or film rights. But this percentage does vary, so make sure you know what your agent is asking for. Most agents will also charge you for photocopying and other office costs. In my view, you would be well advised to pay a good agent this percentage of your royalties. Having an effective agent who is respected in the industry, knows the market and has a network of influential contacts is a mark of your professionalism as an author. And your agent is an important ally, always there to speak up for you and negotiate on your behalf. To be more prosaic, an agent's services are also tax deductible.

The 'Curse' of EPOS

In the good old days it was possible to be grandly vague about Exact Sales Figures. Authors who had a loyal fan base and made a modest income did not worry overmuch about the number of books that were being sold in W. H. Smith's. It was all part of the rather amateurish and charmingly old-fashioned attitude that characterised much of the industry until the 1980s. But times have changed.

Now, every author in the country is exposed to the brutality of Electronic Point of Sale (EPOS) data. EPOS records every sale of a copy of your book, recorded by the till transaction in major retailers in the country. (This does not include small independents, however, which is disappointing if you are popular in your local village bookshop.)

Nielsen BookScan came into being in the mid-1990s, and according to Nicholas Clee, editor of the book industry website and newsletter *BookBrunch*, it is the most sophisticated electronic sales-tracking device available to any industry in the world. It covers sales on Amazon and most of the supermarkets, and represents more than 90 per cent of retail book sales in the UK. It does exclude sales to schools and libraries, but is generally seen as an accurate guide to book sales in the UK and overseas. You can find out your own sales figures from BookScan, if you are feeling strong: the fee is £50 per title. (For more information, call 01483 712222.)

This may not be comfortable reading, but will at least mean that you know how a publisher is likely to view you as a potential money earner. And the fact is that this is likely to be taken into account when a contract is drawn up, and an offer is made for your latest book. However, don't despair. Publishers may be suffering in the downturn, erring on the side of caution and panicking about the rise of e-books, but they are not slaves to BookScan. If your existing books have sold badly, but your new book looks like a potential winner, you will still find a home for it. Editors have not yet surrendered the decision-making process to EPOS.

E-Books

Everything is changing fast in publishing. Keep an eye on the market and make yourself as well informed as you can. At the time of writing (2011), Sony is predicting that e-books will outsell print in five years' time, though others in the industry are far more conservative in their predictions.

What does this mean for authors? Does it undermine our copyright? This is a big issue, but some commentators think it could go either way. A study from two US academics at Brigham Young University in 2010, which looked at the effect of free e-book releases, found that a free e-book release usually led to increased print sales.

Not everyone takes such an optimistic view. Tom Holland, chair of the Society of Authors, believes that publishers' attempt to seize control over electronic rights, locking authors into e-book deals for the duration of copyright, is unfair. For more information, go to the Society of Authors website at www.societyofauthors.org. And for more about the rise of e-books, see Chapter 12: 'Writing Online'.

Judith Murray

Judith Murray has worked as a literary agent with the London agency Greene & Heaton since 1995. Before that, she worked as an editor and freelance editor at a number of UK publishing houses and as a talent scout for translation publishers. The agency's clients include Bill Bryson, P. D. James, C. J. Sansom and Sarah Waters.

'I think writers need agents,' she says. 'Writing is hard and lonely work, and it is good to have someone on your side who knows the business of both writing and publishing. If the writer–agent relationship is a good one, there is no reason why it can't last for the whole of a writer's career. Editors and publishers come and go; publishing companies and imprints rise and fall; often, one of the few constants of your career is your agent. So, when you choose one, do your research (look at websites, check acknowledgements pages in books by your favourite writers to see who their agents are) and find out which agent will suit you and your writing; agents vary greatly in personality, style, literary taste, experience.

'If an agent (or more than one) is interested in you and your writing, meet them, ask lots of questions, be clear about your expectations for your writing and your future career and find out if the agent shares them and if they are keen to help you realise those expectations.

'I love working with the writer and their writing: finding out what makes the writer tick, and looking at how their book works in terms of style, form, plot, character, pace and so on. I love the intellectual satisfaction that engagement with a writer's work brings, but I also take great pleasure in selling a book to a publisher and helping that book reach as many readers as possible.

'Knowledge and experience are very important in my

continued

job. I match-make the writer's material with the right editor and publisher, and, when a publisher makes an offer for a book, then I negotiate the terms of the contract on the writer's behalf. Contracts can be a couple of pages long or ten or more. A contract is a "memorandum of agreement": we negotiate the terms of an offer on the phone and by email with an editor, and then the contract is the written form of the agreement which enshrines those terms. As one of the signatories to the contract (the publisher is the other), writers do need to read these contracts carefully and be aware of what their responsibilities and obligations are. If there are things in the contract that you don't understand, ask your agent about them.

'An agent's role is often that of a representative – many of my writers prefer me to discuss difficult situations and subjects with editors on their behalf. That makes perfect sense to me. Another aspect of the role of the agent is to protect the writer. You try to be their champion, as well as their representative.

'It's important to remember that agents need writers – we are always looking for new talent to sell to publishers. When I first start reading your submission, I always ask myself: do I love the writing? And then, just as important a question: could I sell this? And, when I start making a list of the editors who might be just as interested in your submission as I am, then I will probably give you a call.'

The Deal: The Lowdown

- Take pride in the fact that your book has been accepted for publication; but don't be grateful.
- Get a clear idea what the deal involves, and how issues such as foreign rights are being dealt with. Don't let

the publisher have all rights if you can help it.

- Once negations are under way, let your agent take the lead on this, and don't hassle them while they are negotiating on your behalf.
- *Read the contract!* This is not negotiable. If you take no other single piece of advice in this book, take this one.
- When you have read the contract, be certain that you understand everything in it. If you have any queries, seek clarification before you sign it.
- Do not expect a large advance. Do not expect to give up the day job. Not yet.

CHAPTER SEVEN

Perils and Pitfalls

'Ever tried. Ever failed. No matter. Try again. Fail again. Fail better.'
Samuel Beckett

Though it pains me to write this chapter, it is one of the most important in the book. The perils and pitfalls of being a writer are legion. Your book does not sell; it was never in the shops in the first place; your lovely editor leaves; her replacement hates your work; you run out of ideas; you have a host of ideas, but they are *so* last year; the shelves of high street bookstores are groaning with rubbish fiction; the only books that sell are ghosted for celebrities. Not only do writers have to cope with rejection before being taken on by a publisher, they have to deal with it afterwards. Being 'dumped' goes with the territory. And it was ever thus. Jane Austen was paid £10 by her first publisher, heard nothing for a year, and then was offered the chance to buy her book back.

It's essential to be prepared for the fact that a writing career is unpredictable. The highs are wonderful, but, even when things are going well, you may feel a sense of anti-climax. Getting a book published, for instance, is weirdly undramatic.

Blake Morrison advises his creative-writing students at Goldsmiths to be realistic about their prospects 'With students here – when their first book comes out – I want to say, "It is momentous for you but be aware that nothing much really happens." My agent used to send me a little card on the day that my poetry collections were published. But that was the only recognition there was. You need patience and you need calm, and you need not to be too distracted by the gushing of agents and publishers and the excited talk of film deals and all that stuff. Expect nothing, and then if things happen it is a wonderful bonus.'

What's more, success for a writer is rarely a state of being. There tend to be periods in a writer's career – as there are for some actors and directors – during which they are 'hot'. They may have just won the Man Booker, or have written a successful first book. But this phase doesn't usually last.

'There are so many novelists who have a success and then it all peters out, and so you need a calm pragmatism,' says Morrison. 'Trust your friends and the people whose judgement you value, and what they say. And ignore the world as best you can. It is wonderful when you have a bit of success, but sooner or later you will become unfashionable. You have to weather that one. So it is better just to gently build the momentum.'

This has certainly been my experience. I've won prizes and had hugely exciting career breaks – and I've also been crushed by disappointment. What I've learned is to keep going, and to keep writing. One of the reasons that I wanted to write this book is to pass on some of my experience and to help you to negotiate your way through this minefield. Here is my own story which I hope you will find both an inspiration and a warning.

The Novelist's Tale

Once upon a time, I was a small girl, speccy and bookish, who loved books of all kinds, particularly those with magic in them. I suspect the fact that these stories were actually about witches or fairies or imaginary worlds symbolised for me the magic that all books had inside their covers, and the fact that, every time I read a story, I could escape. For as long as I can remember, certainly since I was five or six, I wanted to make up these stories as well as read them. So far, so typical.

I started with *Narnia*-inspired maps, with mountains and lakes and wiggly coastlines. I invented characters, human and otherwise, and drew pictures of princesses with long curly hair (mine was straight) and no glasses. When I was twelve I wrote my first 'full-length' novel, *The Lords of Eela*, about a schoolgirl called Emma Woodwiss who discovered a lost world by climbing into a chest. She met a family of slightly Arthurian lords and ladies who had been banished to a lost island. It started well, but had rather a flat ending. (They were rescued in a *deus ex machina* kind of way by Neptune and his watery knights.) This story went on for one hundred handwritten pages. When I got bored, I drew a picture.

My second 'novel' was slightly longer – about twelve pages longer, I think. This time it was the story of Moira Odette Thomasina Hazeldine, or M.O.T.H. She was an ordinary school girl, like me, with glasses (highly significant) and plaits (but blonde, not brown like mine). The story concerned her time at a school for witches, supported by her adviser, a talking dove. There was more drama in this one, partly because I introduced some baddies in the person of various teachers at the witch school. Perhaps if I had stuck with this tale of trainee witches, I would have been a multimillionaire by the time I was eighteen. Sadly, I moved on.

I became a teenager, often heartbroken, trying and failing to be cool and writing terrible poems. I knew they were terrible even then; or, at least, I knew they were therapy, which amounts to the same thing. Stories were my thing. But a fizzing, dizzy panic used to loom up when I thought about writing one. I knew I should be doing it, was strangely lost without it, but had no idea what to say. My early twenties were a period of boozing, more heartbreak, a hell of a lot of whingeing and then a sudden determination to do something positive. So I entered the *Cosmopolitan* new journalist award and – as you have already heard – I won. I assumed I had Arrived – a mistake I have made several times since, but not one that I will make again.

Not only had I not arrived, my subsequent failure to become a consumer hackette made my actual life seem even more glum and mundane. I went to journalism school, thinking this might be another way in, but ended up getting a dull job in trade publishing in a prefab in a car park in a boring south London suburb. The managing director was a former Millwall football player with sharp suits and bad teeth. I tried to write a satirical book about working in trade publishing in a prefab in a car park in a boring south London suburb. It was called *Bundles*. (It was the eighties.) But the ideas fizzled out after Page 31, the way ideas do.

And then, finally, I decided to do what had to be done, and began attending a writing workshop in Covent Garden, and began to produce short stories. I wrote them quickly, and they weren't very good, but some were commercial. I was runner-up in another *Cosmo* competition – this time the magazine's short-story award. Once again, I thought I had made it, and once again I hadn't. (They didn't even publish my semi-winning story.) But an agent took me on, and a few of my stories appeared in magazines in South Africa, Australia and the UK. I was runner-up in *another* big competition, the Ian St James. Then I got pregnant with my first child.

I decided that, as my creative life would be at an end once I had produced a baby, I needed to write a whole novel in six months. I bought a lot of lined A4, dreamed up a hard-drinking girl, lost in London, and called her Lucy Glass. Then I began to write, against the clock, in biro, filling up the lines. I wrote on and on and on, with no idea where I was going, but I did come up with a title: *Days of Strong Lager*. The baby got bigger. I began to get heartburn. The stack of pages covered in squiggles of black biro grew higher. It wasn't finished, but I had written six chapters, and my characters were saying stuff and moving about, and there were descriptions of outdoors and indoors, and some jokes. I typed it up on my new computer, and sent it off to the agent.

You will be less surprised than I was that she was not happy with my proto-draft. She tried to be kind – she was a very nice agent as well as a good one – but the truth was that my story sucked. In fact, it wasn't a story at all. It wasn't really anything, just words. My boyfriend Noel opened the letter she sent back to me while I was out, and he left me his own note to soften the blow. I still have it. He told me that I *could* write; I just hadn't got it right this time. And that rejection is not terminal, it is just hard.

Getting Published . . .

I stopped writing for a while after that, mainly because I had my baby, Georgia, and I had been correct in assuming this would be the end of quiet scribbling for some time. My son Declan arrived two years later, and we moved to Brighton. I had to leave my day job with a charity, and began to freelance. We were horribly broke. Desperate for money, I pitched ideas to national newspapers as soon as the children were old enough to go to nursery. I began to write a weekly article on employment in the financial markets for the *Sunday Times*, and regular pieces on careers for the *Evening Standard*. I wrote a monthly column on babies for a baby magazine. I learned to churn words out, but keep them readable and sharp. I learned to meet deadlines. I stopped being precious. And I wrote my first proper novel *The Best Possible Taste*.

This would never have happened if I had not had help. Noel took the children out at weekends, to the seafront or the park, and I would write frantically for a couple of hours, then return to my maternal duties. I loved having small children, but it was a hard slog and without writing as an outlet I think I would have gone mad. Bit by bit, I wrote the book. I did a writing course at Sussex University, shared work with a couple of fellow students and wrote with a more professional, beady eye than I had ever done before. In January 2003, I sent the finished novel off to four agents. Within a month, one of them had taken me on. By April, I had a two-book deal with a major publisher.

My book was a decade-defining romp, full of comedy and drama. It couldn't fail. It was *Bridget Jones* meets *High Fidelity* with *Cold Feet* as its winsome love child. It would be on the big screen in no time at all. I even had a meeting with a Hollywood agent in a chi-chi veggie restaurant on Sunset Boulevard. She even asked, 'Is there a part for Hugh Grant?' Of course, I thought I had arrived. And I was wrong.

. . . and Dropped

My editor 'loved' my novel, but was head-hunted and whisked off to another job almost as soon as she had acquired it. My new editor had 'passed' on the manuscript at her former publishing house. Things pretty much went downhill from there. They changed the title. They changed my name. I hated the jacket. (Of course I hated the jacket.) Eventually, the book came out and around 10,000 copies were sold. This would have been fine in former times, but was not fine now. I did not change the face of British publishing. I was not the new Helen Fielding or Nick Hornby or David Nicholls. I was not the new anything.

We moved to Barcelona for a year. I tried to write the second book. I had decided this had to be about the sex war in the eighties. It was going to be an ambitious, state-of-the-world book, half of it written from the male point of view, and half from a female point of view. It would be massive, a sort of *Golden Notebook* for the noughties. It would have a twenty-year gap in the middle, after which all the main characters would reappear in middle life, and a new cast of young people would be introduced, illustrating the ironic changes in the zeitgeist relating to feminism and the Left. I took no account of the kinds of books that my publisher normally produced. I ignored my relative inexperience, lack of time and general feeling of seeping demoralisation. I would just write a great novel, and solve everything.

I sent a great chunk of this new novel to my agent, so that she could check on my progress before the new editor had sight of it, and she hated it. When she explained why, I had to admit that I could see where she was coming from. It wasn't just unpublishable: it was unreadable. I had that head-resting-on-the-keyboard-and-blood-pulsing-from-the-eyeballs moment that all writers know. Noel reminded me that rejection is not terminal. It is just hard.

I cut the book in half, set the whole thing in the eighties, and started again. Some of it worked. Some of it didn't. And then something happened I had heard of, but never experienced. Writer's block. It wasn't that the page or screens stayed empty – I did manage to write something – but the words were dead. The more I wrote, the further away my book seemed to be. I had made a terrible mistake. I wasn't a writer at all.

Unfortunately, whether I was a writer or not, I was contractually obliged to produce a second novel. I wandered about in Barcelona, drinking coffee and doing a lot of swimming in a beautiful, empty blue pool. I got very fit, and gradually, painfully, I finished the book. We returned to Brighton, to debts and a life that seemed smaller than it had been before. The second book came out, after a fashion. It sold hardly any copies. Nothing official was ever said, but it was obvious that, should I ever happen to write another book, my publisher would probably not be interested. I was back where I had started. Or so it seemed.

People would say, 'Well, you've had two books published, that's pretty good!' The assumption was that this ought to be enough. I had had my chance, and done quite well, and my ambitions had presumably been realised. I was a published author, wasn't I? But the problem was that my ambition had never been simply to be published. I wanted to *be* a writer. I wanted writing books to be at the centre of my life. I wanted to make a living out of writing fiction.

The Second Wave

After a few months, I decided to regroup. I knew the second book had had its faults. I knew the first was written in a rush of naïve passion. I knew that there was a craft to writing, a body of knowledge that I could draw on. So I did two things at once: I became a student and a teacher. I signed up for an MA at Brunel University, and became an associate lecturer in creative writing at the Open University. In the following two years, I learned more about writing novels than I had learned in my entire life. Brunel awarded me a distinction for my MA and a scholarship to study for a Ph.D. I was inspired and impressed by the work of students, and found that I loved teaching. And I began to write another book, a historical novel set in Jacobean London, the story of Shakespeare's Dark Lady.

Is there a happy ending? I would say there is, though the story is not over yet. But my writing life doesn't depend entirely on the fate of this book. And writing is not only about publication. Writing is a process. It is a way of understanding life, and relating to it, and laying ghosts and demons. Writing is about entering another domain. I get the same satisfaction from entering the world of my new book that I had from reading Rosemary Sutcliff or E. Nesbitt when I was eight years old. It is pure pleasure, complete escape. And now, six years after my last novel appeared, I have found a new publisher who loves my book as much as I do. Myriad Editions, an independent publisher based in Brighton, will publish my novel *Dark Aemilia* in 2014. A new door has opened. Publication is a wonderful thing. But even without it, I made this book. And, in some way, this book has made me.

There are perils and pitfalls in writing, but they are just part of the process. I wouldn't say they are part of the fun, but they are inevitable. If you want to read more about this philosophy, Toby Young's *How to Lose Friends and Alienate People* is a good place to start. Young brilliantly charts his own ups and downs, and the way that his career blips have made him one of the best-known names in journalism. His advice is: 'Accustom yourself to failure'.

If this sounds like a counsel of passive acceptance, it is anything but. Young has made his setbacks into springboards to success. You may not have his ebullience and cheek, but you can learn from his resilience.

Writer's Block

One of the greatest perils for any writer is that they will lose their imaginative power, the ability to do the work itself. Writer's block has an almost mythic status, among writers and non-writers alike. It takes many forms: fear of failure, horror of the blank page, lassitude, depression, a loss of faith in the entire process of writing. Writing is such a stabilising and engrossing activity that when you lose the ability to do it – or feel that this is the case – there is no compass for the rest of your life.

And success is no protection against writer's block: some writers may be put off their stride by harsh reviews or rejection by their publisher, but others are wrong-footed by praise, feeling that they can never live up to the expectations that have been placed on them. Writing too little can give you writer's block – you have lost your connection with your work. But so can writing too much – you are stale and tired.

If writer's block strikes, take comfort in the fact that most writers have experienced it in some form. It's part of the territory, like being imaginative, observant, introspective, self-absorbed. Footballers tear their tendons; ballet dancers ruin their feet; writers strain their emotions. Some writers refuse to overanalyse their craft, for fear that they will taint its magic and lose their gift. Ian McEwan is one example. Though he is one of the most famous alumnae of the UEA creative-writing programme, he is not given to scrutinising the various stages of his creative process. He prefers to take country walks and let his ideas germinate quietly.

So there is no shame in being blocked and it doesn't mean you can't write. Quite the reverse: it is almost endemic. On the other hand, don't make a fetish of your stasis or overplay it. See it as the equivalent of a physical injury and work towards getting into a better frame of mind as calmly as you can. Screenwriter Arthur Penn suggests facing up to your demons, believing that we are often blocked because we are evading our deepest fears. Virginia Woolf advises writers to be kind to themselves and stay away from their harshest critics – including internal ones. And Orhan Pamuk says that you need to be patient with your own creative process. A book can take years to write. Rushing to meet self-imposed deadlines increases the pressure, and can lead to cutting corners or refusing to rewrite or rethink when in your heart you know that is what you should do. So don't torture yourself with unrealistic deadlines.

Remember to recharge your batteries. Don't forget that reading is as important as writing. Read for pleasure, let another writer take you into their invented world, and let their words take you over. Don't worry about losing your 'voice' because you are reading someone else's work: in some ways, writing is a conversation between writers. You may feel isolated, but your book is connected to all the other books that exist, and their authors are your colleagues and allies as well as your competitors. Read acquisitively. Getting ideas and inspiration from other writers isn't plagiarism; copying their work is plagiarism. Feed your imagination and wallow in the process.

Fay Weldon

Fay Weldon is the author of more than 30 novels, and a well-known screenwriter as well as a renowned novelist and social commentator. As well as enjoying her success, she has also had to learn to cope with setbacks. Her advice is to keep your eye on the main event – the quality of your writing.

'Best to concentrate on writing good books than with what's going on with your "career",' she advises. 'See it as an art form, not a business. Whether you write Mills and Boon or see yourself as a literary writer, you are engaged in a craft that will slip over into art if you get it right. As to how that's to be achieved, you must rely on your own opinion, not on other people's. And that is hard, because other people have the power to decide whether you are to be published or not. Tact is required.

'Dealing with differences of opinion, clashes of personality takes patience and good judgement. If the other person is right, and they may always be, admit it. Prima donnas quickly make a name for themselves, and it's not a good idea to saddle yourself with a reputation of this kind.

'Best to present yourself as a pleasant and reasonable person, so that when you walk into an agent's or publisher's office they are pleased to see you. Do not become a "difficult" author, which is very tempting, but seldom gets you anywhere, unless you are fortunate enough to be their top seller anyway.

'The knack, I think, is to show yourself to be in defence of your own work, not your own importance. It's a significant distinction; you are your book's advocate. If you don't want to change it, it isn't because you wrote it and so it must be good, it is that you understand it.

'Publishers are now operating in a tough market, and,

continued

though writers may mourn the fact that sales departments wield so much power, this is not going to change. So authors need to have strategies to deal with this. Your editor, no matter how he likes and appreciates your book, now has to go to a marketing meeting and sell your book to them. It's not as it was in the days when the editor had the discretion to decide which books to publish, and could be trusted to do it.

'Few things are as bad as you fear, or as good as you hope. Be prepared for anything. The newly translated author, travelling abroad for the first time, can find it quite alarming. The foreign publisher sends the ticket – you turn up. You trust there will be someone at the airport to meet you. Mostly there is, occasionally there isn't. You must fend for yourself until someone turns up with a schedule. You haven't got the name of the hotel: the details are in your luggage, which has been lost. Or you might find there is a snowstorm, you land miles from where you are meant to be, you are on your own and you have to be self-reliant. Volcano ash falls, things happen, you have to have a bottle of water, a map and a raincoat. You may end up walking for miles in the snow, on your own. Put it down to experience.

'And, if you are being translated while you speak, it is quite distracting. This sometimes happens to me when talking at book fairs abroad. You might have a very inadequate microphone and be talking to people who are walking around and buying books (with any luck) even as you are speaking, or the sound has broken down. Smile and put up with it. Once, at the Danish Book Fair an enormous vase of amaryllises fell on my head from a wobbly pillar and drenched me, and nearly killed me. Did I complain? No. That's public life.'

'While you wait for your life to bloom and blossom all you can do is write the best book you can. And do try to be lucky.'

Perils and Pitfalls: The Lowdown

- Prepare for a long game. Don't assume your first success will change your life.
- Have support networks in place, and listen to the people you trust.
- All writers have disappointments and setbacks. It is not the mark of failure.
- Display grace under pressure and don't play the prima donna.
- Don't panic if you get blocked or stale. There are ways of working through this.
- Write the best books that you can, no matter what else happens.

CHAPTER EIGHT

Day Jobs

'*Faulkner learned his trade while working in the Oxford, Mississippi, post office. Other writers have learned the basics while serving in the Navy, working the steel mills or doing time in America's finest crossbar hotels. I learned the most valuable (and commercial) part of my life's work while washing motel sheets and restaurant table cloths in the New Franklin Laundry at Bangor.*'   Stephen King

In 1938, Cyril Connolly, a writer, journalist and literary critic, wrote a book that set out to analyse the emerging literary scene and explain his own failure to produce a work of genius, in spite of the early signs that he was one of the most brilliant writers of his generation. He identified a number of obstacles to success including journalism, politics and sex, which could lead, he warned his readers, to prosecution for homosexuality, or a permanent entanglement in domesticity and parenthood. The book was called *Enemies of Promise* and from it comes one of the most famous quotes about day jobs ever written: 'There is no more sombre enemy of good art than the pram in the hall.' This sonorous and somewhat melodramatic pronouncement is often used to support the idea that family life and creativity are incompatible.

Writers want to write, but they do not generally live a

hermit-like existence. Even the most dedicated author will fall in love, set up house and buy things. Many get married; some get divorced. All of this costs time and money. Normal Life is expensive. Only a minority of writers earn enough to live entirely from their work, and it was ever thus. So they spend some of the time they could be writing doing something else that brings in regular money. In short, Connolly was concerned about the dangers of the day job.

Grafters and 'Real Writers'

Parenthood is the mummy and daddy of all day jobs, of course, and its great crime is that its demands and responsibilities are endless. In purely rational terms, it would be sensible to keep your living expenses low, and make sure that your writing ambition takes precedence over domesticity. But, if you follow this idea to its logical conclusion, then the only people who could become writers would be those with a private income, or who were prepared to live a monastic half-life, steadfastly keeping all forms of distraction at a distance.

Fortunately, the opposite is true. Most of the great names in English literature were grafters of the middling class, who worked hard at their craft, but were also involved in a host of other activities. This is true of Geoffrey Chaucer, William Shakespeare, Jane Austen, John Keats, Charles Dickens, George Eliot and James Joyce. Even well-bred authors with money behind them led extraordinarily busy and complicated lives: Lord Byron and the Earl of Rochester spring to mind, with Lady Antonia Fraser bringing up the rear.

And yet, in spite of all the evidence to the contrary, the prevailing image of the Real Writer is of someone who is sequestered from the world, and who writes, or thinks, or has lunch with other writers and thinkers, all the time. The focus on best-selling authors has added weight to this idea. Success means giving up the day job. Failure means having to carry on with it. Aspiring writers are often very keen to know how soon they can join this happy band of full-time scribblers, and jack in the day job, saying, in the words of Philip Larkin, 'Stuff your pension!'

Here is the reality check. Even writers who are paid a generous advance at some point in their writing career are likely to find the money has run out, and that there is still a mortgage to pay and children to provide for. As we all know, publishing is more polarised than ever, and in general an author who is already rich and famous is much more likely to be paid handsomely for a new manuscript than an unknown author who is overworked and overdrawn. Read any article about 'the death of the mid-list' and you will find plenty to depress you. In 2005 the Authors' Licensing and Collecting Society (ALCS) commissioned a survey of authors' incomes, and found that the median or 'typical' earnings from writing are just £4,000 a year. You can't even rent a garret for that. Which means most published authors must stick with the day job.

You may blanch at the prospect. The time that could have been spent crafting a narrative must be spent at the call centre, or infant school, or bank. Weekdays will disappear in an endless round of commuting and tedious grunt work. Weekends must be for ever filled with household chores and family demands: shirts to iron, food to cook, bills to pay. Oh to be Ian McEwan, sitting in his Oxford study with fresh flowers on his desk, writing something elegant that sums up the zeitgeist. Or Kate Mosse, cool and pretty, penning a new best-seller in the ancient town of Carcassonne.

I have just two words for anyone wimpish enough to indulge in such negative and defeatist thoughts: 'Melvyn Bragg'. He has written twenty novels, thirteen works of nonfiction, three children's books and four screenplays. He edited and presented London Weekend Television's *South Bank Show* for more than thirty years, and was in charge of LWT's arts output for most of that time. His BBC broadcasting CV includes *Start the Week*, *The Routes of English* and *In Our Time*. Since 1998, he has also been a member of the House of Lords. He also has three children and supports Arsenal FC. Most people would find just one of these activities – with the possible exception of supporting the Arsenal – more than enough to fill a lifetime. How did he manage to write all those books? *Twenty novels?* How does he keep all this stuff in his brain? Where does he find the energy and the motivation? In a recent *Observer* interview, he said, 'I took five, six years off in my late 20s, early 30s to write full time and establish in my mind what I wanted to write. Now I'm one of those people who runs writing alongside a day job. There's a lot of hours in the week if you use them properly.'

Obviously Bragg is fortunate in that he loves his work, and this generates its own energy. This is very different from slaving over a dull job all day and then trying to write in the evenings. But what matters isn't the amount of time that he is able to dedicate to writing, but his attitude to that time. And it is possible – though not easy – to create more energy if you take a different attitude to the daily grind.

Day Jobs – The Good News

Day jobs are useful for two reasons. First, they give you a secure financial framework. It is easier to work on a book if you aren't worrying about how to get to the end of the month without beating off the bailiffs. And, second, they give you something to write *about*.

The career of Raymond Carver is a case in point. He married at nineteen and much of his early life was dedicated to supporting his wife and children, working long hours doing odd jobs for little pay, and fitting in his writing where he could. During this time, he started to drink heavily. Writing short pieces fitted into his hectic lifestyle: he juggled writing with work and intermittent alcohol binges. Even when he gave up drinking, remarried and became part of the literary establishment, Carver wrote about blue-collar life, and about alcoholism and recovery. Without his grinding, irksome day jobs, what kind of writer would Carver have been? Without his sense of exclusion and desperation, what would have fuelled his determination to make his voice heard? I'm not saying that his writing depended on his 'grunt work' but that without it he would have been a different writer, and he would not have produced his stark, arresting stories about the underside of the American Dream.

Having a day job is a way of engaging directly with society. It's a common experience, just like falling in love, fearing death and feeling nostalgia for lost youth. Most adults work for a living, and millions spend a huge chunk of their life either sleeping or doing a job they don't particularly enjoy. Fiction often focuses on dramatic or extreme experiences that offer an escape from the mundane, such as crime, war and romance. This works perfectly well: observe the vast numbers of commuters who are immersed in the latest serial-killer tome on any crowded train. But there is also something to be said for being the sort of writer who has lived the life of a non-writer, and knows what it's like to be stuck on a commuter train, reading a thriller, dreading the day to come.

It's also useful to get away from the job of writing some of the time. Very successful writers have this built into their schedule automatically, in the sense that they are expected to promote their books and often become public figures with all the demands that this involves. But, away from the public gaze, full-time writers can be rather isolated and self-involved, and frequently associate with other writers who are equally solipsistic. They are stuck with a search for significant subjects – subjects worthy of their attention – and with the fear that their associates might be having more literary success than they are (or might be just about to, which is equally unnerving). It can become a neurotic business. There is no scientific measure of whether writers are really any more self-absorbed than car mechanics or IT engineers. Perhaps they just go on about it more. But at its worst a 'writer's life' can spawn literature that is inward-looking and self-indulgent, or that is so keen to address the weighty issues of the hour that it lacks human focus.

The specific details of life are often details we would be happy to do without: the cramped, tedious, repetitive nature of weekday living; the annoying colleagues; the dull feeling of foreboding that looms every Sunday before the working week begins. If we could remove all the discomfort and unpleasantness from our lives, we probably would. But what exactly would we be left with? What would we have to chafe against? And where would we find our material?

For whatever reason, some writers happily carry on with the day job after their publishing career is established. Alaa al Aswany, one of the best-known novelists in the Arab world, still practises as a dentist in Cairo two days a week. It's reasonable to assume he doesn't need the money. His first novel, *The Yacoubian Building*, was published in 2002. A best-seller for five years, it was made into a film and a TV serial, and has been translated into twenty-seven languages.

Finding a Balance

Day jobs aren't necessarily a neat part of the working week that must be dealt with before the fun can commence. They can be as engrossing as writing and – if you're lucky – just as enjoyable. Naomi Alderman, the 2005 winner of the Orange First Book Prize with *Disobedience*, still writes computer games. 'I don't really look at my games writing as my "day job" and my novels as my "real calling",' she says. 'I'm not just doing the games to pay the bills, but because I really love working on them.

'The two kinds of work feed different parts of me. Novels are by their nature solitary and individual. You have total control over what happens in your novel, but that also means that no one else is really in a position to help you make it better. Games are far more collaborative; it means that the vision isn't totally my own, but also that I get to spend my time debating and discussing rather than just pulling my own hair out alone! For me, the two work well together; I'd miss either part if it were taken away.'

So there are good reasons for having a day job of some kind, in addition to bare necessity. But is there such a thing as the perfect day job? Is it possible to choose? You may think not: your career may seem like a series of accidents, happy or otherwise. And the right day job will vary, depending on your personality, talents, education, age and general circumstances.

All day jobs can provide you with material, no matter how dull they seem. (Matt Thorne's first novel, *Eight Minutes Idle*, is set in a call centre; Nicholson Baker's *The Mezzanine* takes place in an uneventful lunch hour.) Some, but not all, might provide you with useful contacts (journalism, publishing and academe all fall into this category). As a general rule, however, I would suggest that:

- it should leave you with enough mental energy to write fiction;
- it should be congenial, and not emotionally draining; and
- it should be permanent, giving you a regular income.

A permanent job may not be easy to find in the current depressed employment market, but I have added this to the list of ideal requirements because for fifteen years I worked as a freelance journalist, and, though I made a good living, I often worked at weekends, chasing tight deadlines, and usually had no idea how long a particular client relationship would last.

What you need, more than anything, is structure and peace of mind. I'll talk about budgeting in another chapter, but do consider working fewer hours for less money so that you can spend more time on your writing. If you work part time, knowing that your income covers your basic expenses, then you're more likely to be able to focus on your writing during the regular time you have set aside for this. You can't have everything. Three years ago we moved to a cheaper house so we could reduce our mortgage and live more economically. In those three years, I took an MA, began a Ph.D. and wrote two books.

For most of us, a day job represents some sort of compromise. One solution is to find a job that is a complete contrast to your writing work and gives you an insight into another world – the law or landscape gardening might be equally useful in this respect. Working outside the publishing field also has the virtue of taking you outside its insular concerns. Personally, I rather like the idea of landscape gardening, and the contrast between tilling the ground and working on a novel. However, the only thing I have ever grown successfully is one self-reliant pot plant, so I teach creative writing.

Looking for Synergy

Teaching creative writing is one of the day jobs that have a synergy with writing itself, which I find extremely useful. Every day, everything I do relates to imaginative writing, in fiction, poetry or for the screen. I'm thinking about what publishers are looking for, about new and established genres of writing and about the bigger issues of literacy, culture and the future of the book. But this doesn't work for everyone – Stephen King says that the period he spent teaching creative writing gave him writer's block. The downside of a job with synergy is that you become obsessive and fixated on writing and publishing to the exclusion of all else, and this can make you feel stale about your own writing. And the coalition government's slash-and-burn approach to humanities subjects – as I write this in 2011 – will not make it any easier to get a job in a university. Even if there are fewer jobs in academe, however, you could still consider setting up a private workshop in your area, or teaching creative writing in schools.

Working in publishing is useful in terms of finding a place for your own writing. Whatever your function, you will meet people who can help you, and you will know what is going on in the industry. Publishing is still a profession in which promotion from junior, administrative roles is a respected route to the top, though most secretaries are now graduates, often with good first degrees. Getting in is tough. Consider a move into publishing only if you are relatively young and are prepared to work hard for little money, at least to begin with. Publishing may once have been a somewhat dilettante profession, but those days are long gone.

The third profession that has a synergy with writing is journalism. Cyril Connolly may have given it the thumbs-down, but a huge number of writers either began as journalists or continue to work in the field after they are published. Like publishing, this is a fertile ground for making contacts and staying abreast of new trends in writing. Journalists are also in the business of producing words on demand, and tend to take a practical, no-nonsense approach to writing fiction. Publishers like this.

Work–Life Balance

Old-school professions such as medicine and the law will earn you the respect of potential publishers, and will certainly pay the mortgage. Both are also good sources of material. A glossy career in advertising, film, fashion or the City will also impress publishers, and, again, they will be excellent material for your work. As a highly paid professional you can, if you are prepared to downshift to some extent, negotiate lucrative contract or consultancy work, so you can establish a healthy balance between work, writing and the rest of your life.

Then there are the administrative or middle-management

jobs, which do not, frankly, set editors' pulses racing as the subject for fiction. (There is still no best-selling literary equivalent of *The Office*, though perhaps there ought to be. The nearest equivalent is Joshua Ferris's 2007 novel *And Then We Came to the End*.) If this is the sort of job you do, keep a notebook, find corners of time where you can, and look at ways of reducing your hours or using some of your holiday for a writing blitz. One poet I know has a window in his computer that he opens to work on his poetry when no one is looking. (He works in an architect's drawing office.)

If you can't afford to work part time, one solution is to work compressed hours. This means putting in a full-time week, but over four days instead of five, so that you have a free day to concentrate on writing.

But a writer may just as easily work as a postman/woman, or a swimming pool attendant. Any job can be a day job. You may be reading this and considering a change of career, with the aim of finding more time to write. This is a perfectly sensible solution, but bear in mind that radical career change takes time and costs money – and that, whatever career consultants might tell you, the older you are, the harder it gets. That said, I changed career in my forties and haven't regretted it once.

An Unsuitable Job for An Author

Another word of warning. Unless you have no responsibilities beyond paying your rent, I would counsel against throwing in your career to wait on tables or find work on a building site so that you can fund your writing habit. These jobs take a lot of physical stamina, and, while a list of offbeat, colourful jobs looks great on the book jacket, they are usually holiday or gap-year employment, not the author's current day job.

I'd also think twice before setting up your own business,

which will absorb you day and night for a good two years, and leave no space for novel writing. On the other hand, once you are established, you might find that you can start to factor in free time for writing. But do bear that in mind if you are reading this book with a redundancy cheque in the bank and trying to decide on your next move. It is likely to be either your novel or new business: trying to do both at once will drive you mad.

The Parent Trap

Novelist Candia McWilliam has said that one baby equals two unwritten books. I think this is a conservative estimate. Parenthood starts messy, and it carries on being messy, and the only way you can be a writer and a mother (or father) is to lower your standards in all areas – unless you have hired help, that is, or are of a brutally single-minded disposition. There is a general feeling (among women) that mothers have the worst of it, but having babies usually means more work in the home for women and more work outside the house for men. Neither of these pressures is conducive to writing fiction. I agree that publishing can be sexist, and that genius is a supposedly a quality of maleness, but I am not convinced that these inequalities are exacerbated by babies. The issue is much wider than that. Childless Virginia Woolf talked about the Angel in the House, personifying the female as a guardian spirit of tranquillity and a pleasant home. What oppresses women is not motherhood, but the idea that femininity and domesticity go hand in hand.

Of course combining motherhood and writing fiction is hard. I used to have not just a pram in my hall, but a huge double buggy, forming a sort of Berlin Wall between me and the outside world. It was the size of a combine harvester, too wide to fit through the door of any shop except the local Co-op. God, how I hated that thing. As if in answer to a prayer, it was eventually stolen from outside our front door when I left it there because the wheels were smeared with dog poo. But it was while that monster lived in the hallway that I began to write my first novel.

Since having children I have worked on my writing little by little. Becoming a mother gave me a reason to try to make something of my writing talent, and also gave me confidence, a sense of being more solid in the world. Of course, it was much harder when the children were tiny, my nights were disturbed and I was woken each day at 5.30, foggy with exhaustion. But the fog cleared, the pages of my book piled up, I learned to work in half-hour bursts, and I kept going.

My advice for writing parents is to aim low, do a little, often, and enlist as much support as you can, in the form of both practical help with childcare and artistic solidarity, perhaps by joining a workshop or meeting regularly with a friend who wants to write fiction. Keep it going. Don't expect miracles, and don't underestimate the immense value – and pleasure – there is to be gained from keeping a journal during these hectic, chaotic but magical years.

One of the hardest things about new and early parenthood is that the order and structure of working life is disrupted, and it's tempting to try to create a new order, and a new structure. But I'd advise some degree of surrender to chaos. Writing is good for that, particularly if you don't try to rush a best-selling novel out before your child's first birthday. Taking this approach may allow you to enjoy both writing and parenthood, and, if you do manage to get a few notes down every day, you will be astonished how much you produce.

I'd also like to say something controversial to new mothers. Get over it, girls. Far too much attention is paid to the early years of motherhood, as if this marked the end of your mental and physical freedom. It might be a hiatus, but your life will soon reorganise itself around children, and, if you want to carry on writing, you will. Books like Rachel Cusk's *A Life's Work: On Becoming a Mother* focus on the first phase of motherhood, which is indeed physically tough and emotionally draining. Society is organised so that many of us live some distance away from our extended family. So, when a new baby comes along, we are on our own, National Childbirth Trust notwithstanding, and it can feel as if these early years will last for ever. But they don't. At five, your child will go to school. At fifteen, they will be out of the house more than you would like. At twenty-five, they may have children of their own. For most of your life you will not be the parent of small children, but of adults. I started writing in my thirties, before I had babies, and now my children are teenagers. They are not under my feet. They do not stop me writing. You can't have it all, but you can have a hell of a lot. And writing is a long, long game. Have your babies, and enjoy them, and get as much sleep as you can.

Top three writer-friendly day jobs – the pros and cons

Creative-writing teaching

PROS: Gives you the chance to eat, breathe and sleep creative writing and dovetails perfectly with a writing career. Your employer will actually want you to write books: your publications attract extra funding.

CONS: Teaching absorbs both time and energy. It can be hard to focus on your own writing.

GETTING IN: Universities ask for a good first degree and higher degree in creative writing. Most now expect new staff to have a Ph.D. as well. Public services cuts will affect humanities recruitment in future.

continued

WRITER-TEACHERS: Fay Weldon, Andrew Motion, Philip Hensher, Joseph Heller.

Publishing

PROS: You will understand what makes a book work, and how the industry functions. And you will have brilliant contacts.

CONS: Salaries are sometimes low, particularly in junior roles, and it's tough to get in. Loving books is not enough: publishing is a highly competitive business.

GETTING IN: You will need a good first degree, determination and a willingness to work hard. A degree in publishing may help, but graduating from a top university is more impressive.

WRITER-PUBLISHERS: Stevie Smith, Charles Dickens, Ken Kesey, Virginia Woolf.

Journalism

PROS: You will be producing words on demand, meeting deadlines and (possibly) making useful contacts.

CONS: It can be exhausting and insecure. The future is uncertain, and Web journalism pays less than print. Salaries vary, in spite of the best efforts of the National Union of Journalists, and big names command higher fees.

WRITER-JOURNALISTS: Georges Simenon, Ian Fleming, Arthur Koestler, Mark Lawson.

Writers with day jobs

F. SCOTT FITZGERALD was one of the most influential American writers of the twentieth century. But only his first novel, *This Side of Paradise*, sold well enough to support his opulent lifestyle. (Not even *The Great Gatsby* could keep him in champagne.) Like most professional American authors at the time, he supplemented his income by writing short stories for magazines and selling the film rights of both his stories and novels to Hollywood studios. (With characteristic self-dramatisation he described such activities as 'whoring', though some of these short stories are classics of the form.)

GEORGE ORWELL is a veritable poster boy for the day job. He worked as a policeman, schoolteacher, bookshop assistant, journalist, radio producer, guerrilla fighter, smallholder and post office manager, as well as trying out hop picking and waiting as part of his research for *Down and Out in Paris and London*. He drew on these various jobs in his novels and memoirs, and (famously) based the dystopian, totalitarian world of *1984* on the BBC, where he was employed to write propaganda for the India Service during the Second World War. He deeply loathed working for the Burmese police service, but used this experience to write one of his most brilliant stories, *Shooting an Elephant*, as well as the searing novel *Burmese Days*. Not only this, the early death of his first wife meant that he was also a single parent.

VIKAS SWARUP has served as an Indian diplomat in South Africa, the UK and the United States, among others, and he's the author of two novels, including *Q&A*, which was translated into forty-three different languages, was

continued

shortlisted for the Best First Book by the Commonwealth Writers' Prize and won South Africa's Exclusive Books Boeke Prize 2006, as well as the Prix Grand Public at the 2007 Paris Book Fair. It was later filmed as *Slumdog Millionaire*. The film won eight Oscars, the largest total won by a single film since *The Lord of the Rings: The Return of the King* in 2004.

In August 2009 Swarup was posted to Japan as India's Consul-General to Osaka-Kobe. His previous postings include stints in Ankara, Washington, DC, Addis Ababa, London and Pretoria. He has also written for *Time*, the *Guardian*, the *Telegraph*, *Outlook* magazine (India) and *Liberation* (France).

Day Jobs: The Lowdown

- The pram in the hall is not the greatest enemy of promise: parenthood is just another day job. Writers write, no matter what else they do.
- Writing isn't likely to make you rich, so be realistic about what your writing life will look like and seek out a day job that is congenial and flexible.
- Some of the greatest writers in the language have led the busiest lives: Shakespeare was an actor, theatre manager and businessman; Dickens was a publisher, journalist and public figure; George Orwell did just about everything.
- Day jobs keep writers grounded and they are a rich source of material and inspiration: Raymond Carver, Nicholson Baker and Joshua Ferris have all written brilliantly about work.
- Don't expect your day job to stay in the background – sometimes it will take over for a while.
- What a writer needs, more than anything, is structure and peace of mind. In the absence of a patron or a million-pound book deal, this will come from your day job.

CHAPTER NINE

Money Matters

'No man but a blockhead ever wrote, except for money.'
Samuel Johnson

Controlling your money will help you protect your peace of mind. And, as you will know, if you want to sustain a career as a writer, you don't simply need to find enough time, but also some degree of mental freedom from petty money worries and daily hassle. Fretting about unpaid bills, outstanding tax demands and a general malaise in your current account is not conducive to creative thinking.

But it is unfortunately true that many writers who handle words with flair and skill fall apart if confronted with anything more numerically challenging than the milk bill. The temptation is to be so busy writing, researching and generally rushing about that there is no time left to sort out your financial affairs. If you are anything like me, this can develop into a continuing lassitude concerning anything to do with paperwork.

You don't need me to tell you that taking up the ostrich position when it comes to sorting out your financial admin is a terrible idea. But I'm going to anyway, because, based on my own experience, this is a bad habit that is hard to break. First, you will become stressed and anxious about the state of your affairs. Your mind will fill with static as shopping bags stuffed with bank statements pile up around you. And, secondly, you will inevitably pay out more money than you need to, in the form of irritants like bank charges, fines imposed by HM Revenue & Customs (HMRC) and pointless direct debits.

Look at your financial affairs as you would look at a new novel. It may be tempting to write 'Chapter One' at the top and plunge into the story, but this inevitably ends in stasis on Page 30. Instead, you need to think about your themes, characters and structure and do at least some basic research.

Getting your finances into some sort of order is like planning and researching a new book. If you put in enough time at the beginning, you will save yourself a lot of trouble later on. Setting time aside for this purpose may make you feel all fizzy and uptight about your work-in-progress, but it's essential, and will mean you can concentrate on your artistic endeavours more happily and spend less time on the boring bits at the end of the financial year. You will also save money, which in turn buys you time to write. So it's basically a no-brainer. You have to do this.

Getting Organised

Buy a lever arch file, filing cabinet or other failsafe, efficient filing system. Research online accounting packages such as QuickBooks and Sage, which are improving all the time, or check online for other packages, including open-source software and freeware. Next, register as self-employed. To do this, you need to register with HMRC, using form CWFI, telephone 08451 154515, or go to www.hmrc.gov.uk. You will need to register as soon as you make any money out of your writing – typically, this will be when you get your first book deal. There are two types of National Insurance that you can register for: Class 2 is payable at £2.40 a week and Class 4 is based on taxable profit levels. Don't worry if you have a day job as well: as long as you declare everything, you will pay the right amount of tax for your fiction writing. You can apply to defer payment of these self-employed contributions and your liabilities will be reviewed later.

Then find yourself a good accountant. Word of mouth is always useful, and you can also ask professional organisations like the Society of Authors and the Writers Guild if they have any recommendations. Firms that specialise in working for writers can be useful, as they will understand the issues about spreading your liability over several years, and the fact that writers' incomes vary considerably from year to year. But it is not essential: most freelancers have similarly unpredictable incomes and accountants are used to helping their clients spread the load.

And, as soon as you start receiving payments, you also need to set up a spreadsheet or start a notebook and record the invoices you send out, the payments that you receive and any work-related expenditure that you make. HMRC insists on records being kept, and it's always helpful to keep receipts. But it is also good practice to keep a record of your spending, either on a spreadsheet or in a diary or notebook. Don't feel you have to keep online accounts if you find this a hassle – the tax office is equally happy with written records as long as they are clear and legible.

An accountant can help you balance your books when you have a variable income by 'averaging relief', which is a means of smoothing out peaks and troughs of income over successive years. This is useful if high profits one year are preceded or followed by much lower profits – and can mean that you can reduce your payments on account in a year in which you earn less.

'By averaging, profits that would have been taxed at 40 per cent can be taxed at 20 per cent,' says Barry Kernon of accountancy firm H. W. Fisher and Company. 'But you do have to consider the National Insurance implications of this

– it's a complex area and you would benefit from taking professional advice.'

You also need to decide whether to register as a freelance sole trader, or set up as a limited company. 'We generally reckon that, for a full-time writer, it is beneficial to set up as a limited company where you make at least £30,000 per annum,' says Kernon. 'You do need to take advice on this when you start. If you do set up a company, you will need to set up a business account, and pay yourself a salary to enhance your pension entitlements.'

A limited company can also be used for averaging out earnings over a number of years, because you can vary the amounts you draw out annually, and you can also reduce the National Insurance payable by drawing a smaller salary and supplementing your income with tax dividends. The potential tax saving on around £30,000 of profit is around £2,000, although remember that you will also need to pay more to your accountant if you set up your own company, as this is a more complicated way of doing business.

Whether you are self-employed or have set up as a private company, you need to:

- keep a record of your income and allowable expenses;
- make a note of any capital items that you buy, such as a new car, TV, PC, lap top or other item of office equipment; and
- ensure that your record keeping is clear and consistent.

Allowable expenses include travel related to your writing, whether by car or public transport; research expenses, including hotel accommodation, as long as you can prove that this is the reason for your trip; expenditure on stationery and other work-related, smaller items; and payments to your accountant. Research can also cover courses and conferences, theatre and cinema visits (you can claim only the cost of your ticket), TV costs (typically, say, 50 per cent of TV licence and

Sky/Virgin subscriptions) and setting up a research library; and, when you are setting up, you can also claim a percentage for relevant items that you already own, such as books in your research library. If an asset is inherited, a gift or bought previously, capital allowances can be claimed on either the current market value or the original cost. One self-employed musician was able to claim a percentage for a grand piano that he had actually inherited.

These expenses also cover the use of your home as an office, which can cover any rooms that are professionally used, and is claimed as a percentage of the overall size of your house. Costs taken into account include rent, mortgage interest, council tax, gas, electricity, insurance and general running costs. Telephone (landline and mobile) costs are likely to be a percentage of your overall use, taking into account that you will also use these to make personal calls. You will normally be able to claim the full cost of broadband, where the predominant use of this is for research or other professional activities.

Other allowable expense items include agents' fees and commissions, secretarial assistance and professional subscriptions to organisations such as the Society of Authors and the National Union of Journalists. Publicity costs are also tax-deductible, including setting up a website and buying copies of your own books for publicity purposes. Talk to your accountant about your particular situation to make sure that you aren't missing anything out.

Your income will include: royalties and advances; lecture fees; public-lending-rights income; sale of manuscripts, notebooks and working papers; grants, awards and prizes; sale of film rights; and merchandising. (This last may prompt hollow laughter if you feel that you are a long way from making money from the equivalent of a Harry Potter T-shirt, but you never know.)

If your expenses exceed your income, not only will you not be obliged to pay any tax at all, you may also be entitled to a refund, and you may be able to offset this against either previous or future profits.

An Inspector Calls: Tax Enquiries

HMRC does occasionally carry out an enquiry into an individual's accounts. These can be random or selected, and HMRC has a window of one year from receipt of the return to open a formal enquiry. This is sometimes known as a 'Section 9a enquiry'. The inspector of taxes will not tell you whether this is a random enquiry, carried out simply to ensure that the system is running properly, or has been specifically targeted at you because something irregular is suspected. He or she will send you a list of questions and set out his or her concerns. If more tax is due, interest will be charged and financial penalties may be imposed – so clearly it's vital to keep your records up to date, and make sure that you haven't carelessly omitted any income. If a serious error is uncovered, HMRC may issue what is called a 'discovery assessment' for earlier years.

An enquiry can be set in motion for a number of reasons, including the following:

- using round numbers in the tax return – this implies you haven't kept an exact tally of your income and expenditure, and have come up with an estimated figure;
- when expenses are high in relation to your income – this arouses suspicion because high expenses will normally indicate a high level of professional activity, which should translate into higher earnings;
- when expenses go up but income goes down – ditto; and
- when the figure you are submitting is exactly the same as the figure you submitted the previous year.

Quite literally, it pays to take care. Penalties can be charged if a taxpayer does not take 'reasonable care' with their tax affairs, and these penalties may be charged where the tax office has issued an incorrect statement and the taxpayer underpays tax instead of informing HMRC about this error, or if an incorrect tax return has been filled in, and tax has been underpaid for this reason. If you have taken 'reasonable care' you will not have to pay such a fine. This is defined as:

- keeping accurate records to ensure the your return is correct;
- checking what the correct tax position is if you don't understand something; and
- informing HMRC as soon as possible if you find that you have made a mistake in your tax return, or overlooked something.

Penalties can be reduced if the taxpayer informs the tax office of any errors or oversights they have accidentally made, helps them to work out the additional tax due and allows them access to their records. Many accountancy firms offer insurance to cover this eventuality, and the Society of Authors also has a low-cost insurance scheme for members. It's important to set money aside to pay your tax bill, but, if you really are in difficulties, you can call the HMRC's Business Payment Support Service, who will review your circumstances and may be able to discuss temporary options such as making payments over a longer period. They can be contacted on 0845 302 1435 but they deal only with new enquiries.

VAT

You are legally obliged to register for VAT if you earn more than £70,000 per year. You have thirty days to register, returns are normally prepared quarterly and you must charge 20 per cent for your services. But, if you have a lower turnover, you may also register – this is up to you. You can also go back four years to claim VAT on capital items and six months for expenses. Writers who earn less than £150,000 can register for the Flat Rate Scheme (FRS), which involves charging clients 20 per cent and they then pay 12.5 per cent to HMRC. Enrolling on the FRS makes record keeping simpler and makes it easier to keep track of your cash flow.

Pensions

Don't assume that providing for your old age means that you have to take out a private pension, and, if you do take out a pension, don't automatically go for a scheme administered by an insurance company. Pensions aren't a panacea: they are financial products; and, as you will know, they are financial products that have let an awful lot of people down in recent years.

'Pension schemes are inflexible, and there are other ways of saving for the future, like ISAs,' says Barry Kernon. 'If you earn more than, say, £50,000 a year, then it is worth looking at a pension scheme as one of your possible options, but the most important thing is to have savings of some kind.

'We actually encourage people to have their own fund managers, rather than just taking out a private pension. You need to get a decent fund manager or stockbroker to do that. But you do need to have a reasonable amount of money to begin with – around £30,000 to £50,000 as a starting point.'

Do take an overview and think carefully about how your future finances will work. You can find out what sort of state pension you can expect based on your past and future National Insurance contributions by contacting the Pension Service at the Department of Work and Pensions. Check this out before reducing your hours if you have a day job and an occupational pension; don't rush into spending more time on your writing if you will pay too high a price in years to come. See 'Ten rules for good time management' in Chapter 2 for more advice about fitting writing around other work.

If you want to talk to a pensions adviser, contact the Financial Services Authority for a list of registered advisers. They will charge a fee, or else take a percentage from the financial services company that sells you a pension, so do bear that in mind. They are 'impartial' only insofar as they are not signed up to a particular organisation. Remember that a pension is not the only option available to you when you are planning your long-term financial security.

Authors' Licensing and Collecting Society

The ALCS is a membership organisation, open to all kinds of writer, and pays out what is known as 'secondary income' to authors, not only for full-length novels and broadcast plays or scripts, but also for chapters and articles. Secondary income includes such things as photocopying, cable retransmission in the UK and overseas, digital reproduction, educational recording and repeat use via the Internet.

The ALCS also campaigns on behalf of writers at both national and international levels, with the aim of ensuring that writers receive fair and adequate payment for the use of their work, and that writers' rights are recognised and respected. It also raises awareness of issues that affect writers.

For more information, go to www.alcs.co.uk or call 020 7264 5700.

Budgeting

Do an annual audit of your overall expenditure and look at the areas where there is leakage in your finances. Credit cards are a key culprit here – the safest bet is to cut up your cards, or have one kept in a secret drawer somewhere for an absolute emergency. Other danger areas include:

- EXTENDED WARRANTIES: These are pushed hard by retailers for the simple reason that they make a lot of money out of them. Avoid shop-bought warranties and shop around for separate insurance cover if you really want this kind of reassurance.
- MONTHLY GYM FEES: These can cost you hundreds of pounds a year. Decide whether you are going to the gym often enough to get value for money, and, if you're not, cancel your membership and go to drop-in sessions instead.
- COFFEES AND TREATS: If money seems to leak from your wallet, keep a record of how much money you spend in a month. You will soon find out what your 'latte factor' is, and may be shocked by your profligate approach to caffeine. Forgo the lunchtime deli, and eat a packed lunch instead.
- MOBILE-PHONE AND INTERNET CONTRACTS: Some or all of this expense is tax-deductible, but can still cost a fortune. Shop around, switch to a cheaper supplier or even consider pay-as-you-go.
- PAYMENT-PROTECTION INSURANCE: You don't need this. Don't take out any new deals, and check your bank statements and cancel any existing arrangements of this kind.
- HOUSEKEEPING: Do an annual audit of your mortgage and home, car and travel insurance as well your gas and electricity suppliers, and change to a cheaper provider where possible.

Thrift

As well as conducting a regular audit, try to get into good spending habits on a permanent basis. If you are naturally extravagant – like me – this may all seem rather like hard work. But remember that the less you spend, the less you need to earn, and the less you need to earn, the greater the freedom you will have to write what you want, when you want. Getting and spending really does lay waste our powers, so cutting out unnecessary expense is a way of conserving your energy so that you can do what really matters.

Here are some frugal suggestions:

- get rid of your car – you'll save money, get fitter and help save the planet; look into car-sharing schemes, which are taking off all over the UK;
- stop smoking – the savings here are around £2,000 a year;
- cut down on drinking alcohol and eating out – drinking less means you will have more energy for writing;
- shop at charity shops and flea markets – both are good places to buy books as well as clothes and household items;
- make a list of what you need, and stick to it, rather than splashing out on impulse buys;
- do your supermarket shop once a week – having it delivered also helps cut down on buying unnecessary treats;
- sell your surplus books on eBay or Amazon Marketplace; or sell them to local second-hand bookshops or see if they will give you credit to spend.

Money Matters: The Lowdown

- Register as self-employed, even if you have a day job. You will need to treat your fiction writing income as a freelance income.
- Find a good accountant, via word of mouth or through organisations like the Society of Authors and the Writers Guild.
- Get organised and keep consistent records of your income and spending.

- Don't waste money, either through greed or incompetence. Remember that money is time: time you can spend writing.
- Keep track of everyday expenditure. Write down what you spend for one week to see where your bad habits lie.
- Think long term – if you are reliant on freelance work for your income, make sure that you have a pension or an equivalent savings plan to keep you in your old age.

CHAPTER TEN

Opportunities

'I have always wanted to explore different ways of writing, and stretch my technique. I wouldn't want to be just "the ghost story writer", for instance. I'd hate to be the kind of writer who only did one thing.'

Susan Hill

Getting a first novel published may not change your fortunes immediately. But it will mark the beginning of a new phase of your life. Your book now exists, and your achievements in writing it and getting it published speak for themselves. What's more, there are career possibilities now that did not exist before you were published. They are not always easy to find, but if you combine persistence with hard work you may find some new doors opening to you.

I've already talked about creative-writing teaching – a useful day job for many writers. Being published doesn't necessarily mean you will automatically walk into a teaching job, but it will make you eligible for such a role. Freelance journalism, the other day job popular with authors, may also be more accessible to you than it was before you were a published writer. However, both careers are competitive, and have been adversely affected by the economic downturn. There are a lot of people who would like the security of an academic job, or the kudos of writing literary journalism. It is wise to think laterally about what you might do in future. We live in uncertain times, the 'job for life' has gone for ever, and the Internet has had a huge impact on the jobs market. There are ways of earning a living that didn't exist before.

The most sensible approach to take is to research your options, ask around and see what you might be able to do. Don't expect anyone to tell you what the next move is, and don't expect to breeze into a new role without a lot of effort. But it's also a mistake to underestimate what you have to offer. There are tens of thousands of people out there who have written unpublished books. You have succeeded in getting yours into print. That most brutal of all tests has been applied to your work: commercial viability. There is no doubt that, if you can write to that standard in one field, you should be able to write to a professional standard in another. A word of warning: there will be plenty of threshold guardians anxious to keep you out. You will not be welcomed with open arms. The 'creative industries' are insecure, overpopulated and ruthlessly competitive. You've shown you have the guts and tenacity to write a book – now you have to apply the same dogged determination to making the most of your related talents.

Screenwriting

If you want to write for the screen, you will be up against some of the most ambitious and single-minded people working anywhere. There is less TV drama on our screens than ever before, and the British film industry is facing an uncertain future following the abolition of the UK Film Council and cuts to funding for the arts overall. But focus, hard work and talent will out, so don't let the fact that it will be tough put you off. Look for opportunities and don't be cast down by rejection.

When I lived in Barcelona, my ten year-old daughter was a member of a drama group in the Gothic quarter, and she was hired to cry on the soundtrack of a horror film. Fearing that it might be a little upsetting for her, I went along to the studios and sat in on the recording (which was fine, and she was commended in Catalan for her exemplary weeping). Deciding to maximise my opportunity, I then tried to persuade the film company to make a movie based on my first novel, setting it in the cool suburb of Gràcia rather than in my home town of Brighton. They appeared to have a lot of money, and were making films of astonishing terribleness, so I thought I might be in with a chance. I had a slightly surreal meeting with a Spanish director and an English interpreter, but nothing came of it. However, I certainly learned from the experience (not least that persuasion is easier when you speak the same language). Since then, I've worked on a film treatment for a short horror film, adapted the date-rape chapter of my second book into a short film and co-written the pilot episode of a comedy drama.

Writing for film is extremely challenging, and I would advise you to either start with TV or go the whole way and make your own low-budget movies if you really are serious about this. It's easier than it has ever been to make a film on a shoestring budget, and most independent directors write their own scripts, or use people they already know and trust. If you have a showreel as well as a script, you can demonstrate that you are taking the medium seriously. No one assumes that novelists can write scripts. Nick Hornby has successfully made the transition, but being a good prose writer is not the same thing as being a good screenwriter: you will need to show that you have gone back to first principles and understand the craft.

Don't make the mistake of thinking that screenwriting is just dialogue with pictures attached. It is image-based story telling. You need to think in those terms, and understand that dialogue is just one ingredient. Writing for TV is slightly easier, in the sense that TV scripts are more dialogue-driven, while writing for radio has more in common with writing for the page, though in this instance you need to think about your drama in terms of nonverbal sound as well as what your characters say.

An excellent place to start if you want to write for TV is the BBC Writersroom (see www.bbc.co.uk/writersroom). It used to be possible to write freelance episodes of its daytime soap *Doctors* and I was just about to send in an episode for about two years. Then they changed the system, and now you can send unsolicited TV scripts *only* to the Writersroom. As with any slush pile, there is the awful sense that your work will be read only by a junior person who will skim their eyes over the first few pages and then send you a standard rejection note, but the BBC assures would-be contributors that they will get a serious reading. It is definitely worth trying, and, if you are one of the lucky few, they will put you in contact with a suitable producer.

Writing for Radio

This is still the 'soft underbelly' in terms of getting commissions, as Radio 4 still broadcasts a wide range of drama of all kinds including continuing drama, one-off plays, sitcoms, sketch comedy and family entertainment. Frequently, this is the work of new or unknown writers. Radio is a fascinating and rewarding medium to write for in itself, and success in this medium has led to TV slots for a number of comedies including *Goodness Gracious Me*; *Knowing Me, Knowing You*; and *Little Britain*. Radio drama can attract as many as half a million listeners, which can be a useful way of publicising yourself to potential readers of your books. Writing in one medium can boost your profile in another.

Around three hundred hours of radio drama are commissioned every year, mostly by the BBC. As for TV, you can send your work to the BBC Writersroom, or else submit your script direct to a producer (see *Writers' & Artists' Yearbook* for more information about this). As for writing, you should make yourself an expert in the field by familiarising yourself with what is already being broadcast. You need to understand the potential of the medium and you also need to know what's current and what commissioning editors are looking for.

Read *Radio Times*, which lists the producers and writers of its radio dramas, and get to know the style and approach taken by individual producers. If you praise one of their recent plays in your covering letter, it will do you no harm. Producers are only human, and it shows that you have taken the trouble to do your homework. The standard of radio drama broadcast by the BBC varies enormously. In my view, much of what is broadcast is playing safe and lacks originality. Producers will say this is because they are aiming at a mainstream audience and most listeners will baulk at experimentation or difficult subjects. But, when I heard Lee Hall's great play *Spoonface Steinberg*, I stopped what I was doing and sat down at the kitchen table, completely spellbound. In case you haven't heard it, it's a story told from the point of view of a seven-year-old Jewish girl with autism who is dying from cancer. It's sad and funny in equal parts, and the voice of the child is astonishing. I listened intently, hardly daring to breathe, tears pouring down my face. It turned out I wasn't the only person to respond in this way: the play made Hall's name, and he went on to write the film script for *Billy Elliot*.

Ghostwriting

The majority of ghostwriters start life as writers in another field – often journalism. Their ghostwriting career often begins as a result of serendipity: the journalist interviews an interesting subject, either a celebrity or someone with a good story to tell, and they then approach an agent or a publisher with a proposal for a book. Once you have a name for ghostwriting, you may be approached direct to write a celebrity memoir, or pitch for the work alongside a number of other celebrity 'ghosts'. (When Gordon Ramsay's autobiography was commissioned, rival publishers bid for the work, and each bid included a selection of ghosts so that he could choose whom he wanted to work with.) So it's not that easy to start if you don't have any contacts. But if you have an ear for dialogue and an eye for a good human-interest story, and can write a persuasive pitch synopsis, it's worth a go.

The trouble with starting out if you are not already established is that an agent will want to see evidence that you can do this sort of writing. They may see your novel or poetry as proof enough, but they may want to see something more closely related to ghostwriting. One way around this is to write the book first, if you can find a contact with a human-interest story, and then pitch the finished book.

Book Reviewing

It's not easy to get work as a book reviewer, not least because many of the review pages in the national press have recently been cut. As with ghostwriting, if you want to get this kind of work, you have to get out there and pitch for it. Offer your services to local radio or your local press in the first instance. Also, do some online research and see if there are any openings with e-zines or literary fan sites (see more on writing for the Internet in Chapter 12). Becoming an expert on a certain genre can help, and developing a voice that is recognisably 'you' is also important. It's unlikely that you will be paid for online reviewing, but this can help you create a portfolio that may lead to paid work for a newspaper or literary magazine. Even if you do land a plum reviewing job, it won't pay well. This is something that you do for the glory, and to add to your impressive writing portfolio.

Travel Writing

Again, you will not get rich writing travel pieces, but you might attract new readers if you produce lively, accessible travel articles for newspapers or magazines. There are more outlets for travel writing than for literary reviews – perhaps literature's loss has been travel's gain. Certainly, there is a wide readership for travel pieces that showcase the wonders of exotic places or have a quirky take on travel. Like food writing, travel journalism is aspirational as well as offering useful information. Most people who read your piece on a month in Tibet will be off to Torquay for their holidays. But they can still dream.

Cast your net widely, look at online and specialist publications as well as the pages in the Sunday supplements, and think of unusual angles and ways to 'spin' your travel tales. One friend of mine sold a number of stories to the *Sunday Times* that gave an account of her holidays in South Africa and Malaysia with her four children. This is a field in which elegant, witty, descriptive writing makes all the difference: your skill as a novelist will be put to good use. And, if you get it right, it could even lead to a commission for a nonfiction book, thought celebs like Michael Palin and TV tie-ins do tend to dominate the market.

Don't limit your search to newspapers and glossy magazines. Lonely Planet, Rough Guides and the AA all update their guides regularly and use a host of writers to fill their pages. As with book reviewing, having a niche area that you are really knowledgeable about can help. Brochures and advertorials may seem like the mundane end of the market, but they often pay extremely well. And webzines are a good way of getting started, so that you have something to show other commissioners.

Computer Games and the Graphic Media

You don't need to be young and geeky to write for this sector, but you do need to be a fan of computer games. If you don't enjoy games or are unfamiliar with the latest technology, then you'll find the gaming world confusing. If you want to learn more about video games, buy or rent a console and a few game magazines and get stuck in.

Fantasy writers, science-fiction writers and scriptwriters all have an advantage in the gaming industry. Writers play many different roles in video-game development, including plot, setting, character development, storyboards and scriptwriting. Most games have cinematic sequences that move the game along as the player progresses. But don't expect to start writing games right away – start by writing about the industry, which will help you develop contacts as well as your skills and knowledge about this area.

To find out more go to www.howstuffworks.com/3do2.htm. And to find out more about writing storyboards and scripts for games, read Paul Garrand's *Writing for Multimedia and the Web*.

Deborah Moggach

Deborah Moggach is the author of sixteen novels, including The Ex-Wives *and* Tulip Fever. *She has also written short stories and a stage play, adapted a number of her novels for television and written several film scripts, including* Pride & Prejudice, *which was nominated for a BAFTA.*

'There has been an element of chance in my career,' she says, 'but perhaps less than other people that I know. What I feel more than that is that – like a lot of other writers – I am going to be found out one day. Someone will tap me on the shoulder and say, "You can't get away with this." I don't like anyone to know what I am doing till I have written the whole book – I don't want anyone looking over my shoulder and telling me what they think I should do. So I have always worked on a book till it is ready, and then offered it. I still work in that way. I began by supporting myself during this period with freelance journalism, and later I was able to earn enough from writing fiction or screenplays to fund these periods.

'I wrote a novel in the eighties called *Porky*. It was a story about incest, a very strong and strange novel, and one of the books I have written which felt almost as if it came from somewhere else. I thought it might do a lot of good for people to read it, and thought it could do well. It was published by Jonathan Cape. But they neglected it – I know people always say that, but I have had very different experiences with other books. Afterwards, the editor did say that she had taken her eye off it. So I thought, To hell with all this – I'll write screenplays, and make money and have fun with some actors instead of this.

'Screenwriting is not easy, but I have quite a narrative head and I am good at stories, so that helped. And I do have a visual sense – I draw as well as write. My experience of screenwriting has been very positive, in that when you are writing a novel it is very isolating, whereas screenwriting is collaborative. That can be a problem if you don't like the people you are working with and you think their ideas are rubbish, but, if you are working with people you get on with and throwing ideas around, then it's good fun.

'I do write every day. If I don't I feel nauseous, ill and ratty. I have to. I have to earn a living. Both my parents led by example in this respect – they both wrote every day. My father would write on Christmas Day.

'All the writers I know work extremely hard, and many do masses of hack work to keep themselves going. Not a new thing – but it is tougher than when I started. I got my first book published very easily, and when it came out it was reviewed by all the papers the following week. Nowadays, there may be interest in a first-time author, but it really is difficult when you are bringing out a second or third novel. The last image anyone should have of writers is that it is an easy life, or that we work in a leisurely way.'

Opportunities: The Lowdown

- Getting a novel published is exciting but don't expect it to change your life. What it can do is make it possible to earn your living in a different way.
- You need to make this happen, not wait to be offered writing jobs in other media.
- Possible spin-off jobs include screenwriting, writing for radio, ghostwriting, book reviewing and travel writing.
- Competition is tough for any of these roles, so you'll need to be determined, hard-working and thick-skinned.
- Research the market, and find out if your writing style is a good fit for other forms and genres.
- Look for synergies, and remember that success in one field can boost your profile in another.

CHAPTER ELEVEN

How To Be Your Own PR

'All publicity is good, except an obituary notice.'   Brendan Behan

One of my mistaken assumptions about the life of a published author was that at last I would be allowed to be slightly strange and introverted. For many years, I laboured at the coalface of business-to-business journalism, churning out words to fill in the space around advertisements for dual-action mopping systems and other dark satanic items. I had to wear a suit (a cheap one) and interview the owners of fixtures-and-fittings factories in places like Worksop and Daventry, and try to think of things to say to salesmen and smoke an awful lot of cigarettes. Above all, I had to 'present' like someone I was not. Someone extrovert and normal.

When news came through that I was to be a Published Author, I naturally assumed that my mundane past was now irrelevant. Being published meant that I was free of corporate life for ever. No more suits. No more forced conversations. No more bright smiling mask of fake professionalism. Instead, I could look forward to a pleasant future of quiet contemplation and gentle scribbling, with the occasional liquid lunch thrown in.

I was wrong, of course. Publishing is political, just like any other sphere of life. Publishing is full of hierarchies, and players, of people who are on the way up, and people who are on the way down. Put simply, if you want to be your own PR, this checklist is your starting point.

- If you are of the foot-in-mouth tendency, as I am, think before you speak.
- Be sociable – at least until you have published several solid best-sellers.
- If you do have charm, ebullience and charisma, exploit this.
- Invest in some decent outfits.

As you may already have surmised, your responsibilities as a writer are not over when you finish a manuscript. The job of writing is – to a degree uncongenial to many writers – also a job of selling. At the very least you should be prepared to read your work in public, talk to the reading group in your local library and speak on the radio – so try to string words together with all the eloquence you can muster.

You don't have to go as far as Kathy Lette, one of the great extroverts of the publishing world, who once sat in a book-shop window signing books in her bikini. But don't come over all mean and moody and hope that your enigmatic silence will be enough. It almost certainly won't be. Book signings and book festivals are more popular than ever. Like it or not, we are in an age when readers like to meet authors, and get to know them. Social media like Facebook and Twitter have their part to play – more on this later. But, for many readers, there is no substitute for seeing the author in the flesh.

Celebrities like Katie Price have become best-selling authors. This doesn't mean that in order to become best-selling you must turn into Katie Price, but you do have to make an effort. You may not be a 'sleb' – and you probably don't want to be one, either – but you do need to use whatever comes to hand to raise your profile so that potential readers know who you are, and what kind of books you write. Dotti Irving set up her PR agency Colman Getty in 1987 after working in publishing for many years. Her experience with publishers like Penguin has stood her in good stead, and she has a shrewd and pragmatic view of a fast-changing industry. Currently, her clients include J. K. Rowling and Nigella Lawson, so she is used to managing publicity for writers with a giddyingly high profile.

But what of lesser mortals? What words of advice does she have for writers like you and me, who live our lives well below the public radar? There is a tendency for unknown authors to assume that publishers are interested only in those new writers who are young and good-looking. Be assured that, while they are only too delighted if an author is easy on the eye, the reason for the general air of excitement surrounding a gorgeous, pouting author is that they are a scarce commodity. Most authors look extremely ordinary. Some of the greatest names in literature were positively ugly – there would have been no beauty-pageant prize for George Eliot or Dr Johnson, for example. And, even if we take into account the fact that ours is an age that overvalues youth and beauty, a flick through the book pages of any newspaper will show that homeliness is no barrier to publication.

Having set aside any insecurity you may have about your age and physical appearance, the first requirement is realism, says Irving. You must understand what you can expect from your publisher in terms of publicity, and what you can't.

'Most publishing houses have very good in-house publishing departments, but a lot of them are just far too busy. There are too many books coming out to deal with.' Authors are as notorious for moaning about the amount of publicity they get as they are for loathing their book jacket – and, yes, I am guilty on both counts. But it is far better to be forewarned, and to understand the nature of the business you are in. In a crowded publicity schedule, in a large publishing house, you will be lucky to get the full attention of one person for one day (unless you have written what is referred to as a 'lead title', which means a book they have bought for a large sum of money and are promoting as a priority). This is not because your publisher doesn't believe in your book, or like your writing, or because they are part of some sinister plot. It is just how it works. The rest has to come from you, unless you have the funds to hire an outside agency to help.

That doesn't mean being passive and simply leaving the publisher to get on with it. Irving suggests being as positive and assertive as you can, and making sure that the publicist has all the relevant information that he or she needs.

'This is about having the confidence that what you have brought to the deal is the most important thing – you have written the book,' she says. 'You may not know about marketing, but it is your book, and people have got to respect that. Don't be fobbed off by anybody: agent, publisher, publicist, anyone. But don't do the "anxious author" bit, which is so irritating.'

Instead of agonising about small details and wasting people's time, go through this checklist before making contact:

- Know what you want. Write it down.
- Be realistic about what you are asking for.
- Be specific. Do say, 'You said there would be a book launch – what's happening about this?' Don't say, 'I'm just feeling generally a little bit worried about how things are going.'
- Be professional at all times – this is business.

'What is very helpful is to talk to the publicist and give them some information about you or your writing or where the book came from,' says Irving. 'For example, give them information about where it is set, give them hooks to work with.

'Quite often, people are really unaware of the interesting things they could use, and you need to have a conversation with them to work it out. Authors say things like, "Doesn't everyone write from two till five at the bottom of the garden?" Everyone has something interesting or unusual about them. It is just about finding what that nugget is.'

Another important tactic is to let your publisher know what other sorts of writing you can do. This includes online writing such as blogging – of which more later – and more conventional articles and features for magazines and newspapers, both local and national.

The local media are important to any author – don't overlook this or think they are too small-scale to be relevant. All publicity is relevant. 'Get local bookshops on board, and sign every copy of your book,' says Irving. 'Then it cannot go back to the warehouse. And talk to them about a local author display.' Radio is another good source of local publicity. I was a guest on a version of *Desert Island Discs* at BBC Southern Counties, which was great fun, even though I got to play only five songs rather than the eight you get on the real thing on Radio 4.

Media Training

Not everyone feels comfortable with being interviewed for press or the broadcast media. If you feel nervous, it might be worth investing in media training, or seeing if your publisher can help.

'Some writers are quite internalised, quite modest, while others are the complete opposite and just love to talk about themselves,' says Irving. 'What you want ideally is to be somewhere in the middle, with the three key points that you want to make. Whatever you are asked, you always get these points across.

'Then there are little things like don't wear stripes on the TV and don't wear jangling jewellery on the radio.'

The other key point to remember is that the journalist is not your friend. However, most journalists are good at seeming as if they are: 'putting you at your ease' and encouraging you to open up and reveal as much of yourself as possible. Caution is the watchword here. 'Do be careful, especially in relation to your privacy,' says Irving. 'It will come back and bite you. Don't say things that you don't need to say.

'And don't be afraid to say, "Sorry, I don't understand your question; can I come back to you?" Avoid saying things you don't believe. Try to be slightly in control of the situation, rather than letting the journalist take control. Don't let it run away with you.'

Getting Reviewed

A traditional element of book publicity has always been the reviews sections of newspapers. At the time of writing, books pages were being dramatically culled, and the focus on cost cutting in the mainstream press has seen literary editors lose their jobs.

Is this a hammer blow for authors? Not necessarily. Good reviews don't necessarily translate to high sales, and, at the literary end of the market, the world of reviewers and book pages has always been elitist and (generally) the preserve of metropolitan cliques. As Suzi Feay put it in an article in *The Author*, 'It sometimes felt as though the literary world was crammed into a bell jar, and we were all writing primarily for each other.'

But Feay – who was literary editor of the *Independent* for eleven years – does make an important point: 'Part of the brief of the books pages was to shout about books that weren't by celebrities, and didn't sell into Asda or benefit from 3-for-2 promotion.' The fact that there are now even fewer outlets of this kind makes it even harder for quirky, non-genre and mid-list fiction to get onto the radar.

If you are not part of the literary scene, the chances of getting reviewed on the pages of the national press are pretty small. It's easier to publicise a nonfiction book than fiction, because the actual subject of your book can be used to promote it, and it can also be marketed via the specialist media in its field. Fiction, on the other hand, is more likely to be marketed using the author's existing track record, or the fact that they are an exciting newcomer. Again, give your publisher all the help you can, but don't lose heart if there is a deafening silence in the books pages. Follow up the avenues outlined above, be flexible and think laterally, and remember that some of the biggest literary successes of recent times have come about through that most elusive but effective marketing network of all: word of mouth. This is true of the first or breakthrough books of Helen Fielding, Nick Hornby, Stieg Larsson and J. K. Rowling.

The good news for new writers is that there is a much better chance of getting reviewed online. Small publishers on a limited budget can get a buzz going around an unknown author by organising an 'online book tour', in which the author pays a virtual visit to literary websites and blogs over a specific period of time. Larger publishers are also keen to make the most of online publicity, so do discuss this with your publicist, particularly if you have any recommendations about relevant sites and bloggers. There are also a number of sites that review books of various genres and can help showcase your work, including *Book Chick City* (www.bookchickcity.com) and *Lovereading* (www.lovereading.co.uk).

Literary Festivals

Fiction may not be the new rock and roll, but the publishing industry is following the music industry's lead in that there are more and more opportunities for readers to see their heroes 'live'. In the music business, falling CD sales have led to a greater emphasis on live performance. Equally, uncertainty about the future of conventional publishing has contributed to the current proliferation of literature festivals of all kinds. This is a chance for you, a professional author, to promote your work. There are currently more than 100 different literary festivals taking place throughout the year in the UK, and in most areas of the country, and many are growing each year. In 2010, for instance, *The Times*/Cheltenham Literature Festival reported a 4 per cent increase in ticket sales, taking sales to 120,000, up 5,000 from the previous year's event.

The largest ones include: the *Sunday Times* Oxford Literary Festival; the *Telegraph* Hay Festival; Edinburgh International Book Festival and the Cheltenham Festival of Literature. There are also festivals celebrating a particular genre or type of writing, such as the Harrogate Crime Writing Festival. Allied to this are a number of new events that are associated with music festivals (and which may represent an attempt on the part of publishers to make writing a little more exciting in terms of public performance).

These include the Literary Death Match – 'adversarial readings with a deliberately chaotic feel' according to a *Guardian* article published in August 2010 – and the Shoreditch House Literary Salon, which claims that 'not since the Marquis de Sade has reading been this sexy'. Other new events include the Book Club Boutique, Homework, To Hell with the Lighthouse, Bookslam, the Firestation Book Swap and 5x15.

Unlike the rather county, old-school approach favoured by traditional literary festivals, these are often run in inner-city areas, and are influenced by similar US events, such as the New York-based story-fest the Moth.

So, as in other areas of publishing, change is in the air. You need to familiarise yourself with the territory and find out what is going on in your area both geographically and in terms of subject and genre. The major festivals are dominated by big-name authors, but smaller, local festivals may well be interested in hearing from you. Attend festivals of all kinds, to see how it is done, and how authors present themselves. Then make a hit list of festivals at which you might read your work, go onto their websites and make contact with the organisers. The best way to get on their radar is to tell them who you are and what you are doing. You can also let your publisher know about relevant festivals that you would like to speak at – an approach from them might be more productive than an approach from you. But it is always worth making the first move. Don't just wait to be asked.

Two useful sources of information about festivals are the British Council (www.britishcouncil.org – you can search for festivals from its home page) and Literary Festivals UK (www.literaryfestivals.co.uk).

Giving a reading

Once you have got your booking, the next challenge is to make the most of it. The problem is that, while music naturally lends itself to live performance, writing doesn't. Most of us are not equipped with the storytelling skills of an itinerant troubadour, and hearing a well-known author read an extract from their work at Hay-on-Wye is not comparable to seeing Blur at Glastonbury, even if that author is as charming as Nick Hornby or as cool as Zadie Smith. Which may go some way to explain the fact that non-writing celebrities feature on the programmes of many of the best-known festivals – a trend that started when Bill Clinton rocked the tents (or something) at Hay.

However, your job is not to wish that you were Lady Gaga, but to make the most of what you've got. The key to giving a good public performance is preparation. Ask the organisers how long you have, who else will be speaking (if it is a panel event) and whether there is any general theme. (You might think that you would always be told all these things as a matter of course, but you would be wrong.) If you are giving a reading, choose two or three extracts that can stand alone, that sound good and that will not test your dramatic powers too much. (I avoid reading from the section of my second book that features a feisty New York editor, for instance. I recently heard Toby Young doing some impressive accent work at a meet-the-author session, but I am not Toby Young.)

Don't commit the cardinal sin of many authors, which is to read out far too much. Audience attention spans are short, and most people would rather ask questions and hear your answers than listen to lengthy extracts from your novel. At a literary event in my home town – called the Brighton Moment – around twenty authors read their work aloud. Each one was asked to write a piece about life in Brighton that was no more than nine hundred words long. The short and varied reading went down a storm.

Once your reading is over, try to take the audience's questions in a relaxed, leisurely way. Don't strive to be hilarious, but be human, and, if humour comes naturally, then fine. Remember that there are no wrong answers to these questions; it's not an exam. While it is obviously not possible to prepare for every question that comes up at a Q&A session, do have some answers ready for the most common queries, which will be as follows:

- Did you always want to be a writer?
- Do you have a daily writing routine?
- How did you get an agent and/or publisher?
- Where do you get your ideas?
- Which writers do you admire?

They will also (possibly) ask specific questions about your books. Preparing yourself does not mean scribbling out screeds of notes: just write down a few bullet points on a card to jog your memory.

Finally, while it is not necessary to be a Great Beauty to be a successful author, it is advisable to look as if you have brushed your teeth. Grooming is important, and writerly *dishabille* can very easily segue into something tramp-like.

Men: abstain from jeans and a T-shirt unless you are under thirty and determined to look challenging. Iron your outfit if humanly possible. Women: try to think beyond black unless you are Jacqueline Wilson. Limit clutter, such as scarves and beads. Bear in mind that a skirt that is fashionably knee-length when you're standing will ascend crotch-wards when you sit down.

Take all this into account – and stay out of the hospitality tent till it's all over – and you can relax and enjoy your own show.

Patrick Gale

Patrick Gale's first novel, The Aerodynamics of Pork, *was published in 1985. Since then he has written fourteen novels, including the critically acclaimed* Rough Music, *and a number of short stories.*

'I was always a slow-burn sort of author,' he says. 'I plugged away at it, I produced the novels just regularly enough for my slowly growing body of readers to come to expect them and even anticipate them. And I have never underestimated the importance of recognising readers. Not in what I write – because I write in a sort of bubble, I think – but in the intense pleasure I get from reading in public and doing Q&As with readers at book festivals.

'This isn't just about self-marketing. Writing is an incredibly lonely, obsessive occupation and actually getting to meet readers, especially happy ones, reminds you that the process is mutual, that writer and reader form a charmed circle of two and that every reader will slightly change your book just by all the fascinating personal baggage they bring to their reading of it.

continued

'Then there's the performance side. When I was first published, in 1986 or so, writing was still a profession where you could hide away; but, now there are on average two book festivals a week in the UK alone, I'm sure it would damage your standing as a writer if you refused to take your book on the road at least occasionally. Not many Salingers around now. All the acting experience I got as a student helped, I think. Faced with my first bookshop event, some time in the late eighties, I found that I enjoyed the performance aspect of it and that the audience responded to me.

'I think that has probably helped my "career" as much as the bits of luck that helped keep it afloat initially – if you perform confidently and can make readers feel they've formed some kind of connection with you when they come to your events, word soon spreads among publicists and festival organisers and bookshop owners. But, more importantly, among readers.

'At the risk of sounding like Joan Crawford (who used to make a point of taking the fans queuing outside her house trays of coffee and cookies), I think once you've built a readership and won its trust you can tap into the sort of unofficial word-of-mouth support for your work that no amount of marketing budget can match. And I take that side of things very seriously. I've always had letters from readers – I think that's inevitable when one writes about relationships and "private" stuff – and I've always made a point of responding to them, even the negative ones.

'These days, of course, it tends to be emails. When readers post comments on my website's message board or reviews on its book pages I always respond. It's a bit of a risk – I use my one and only email address to do it – but I can tell from their reaction when they hear from me that it's a risk worth taking.'

How to be Your Own PR: The Lowdown

- Remember that you need to sell your book as well as write it.
- Don't fret about your appearance – just dress smartly and get on with it.
- Be clear about the amount of publicity you are getting from your publisher, and ask how you can help.
- Think local as well as global: make as many contacts as you can.
- Go to literary festivals, and contact the organisers to see if you can be involved in future events.
- Before giving a reading, rehearse your 'act' and have some answers ready to respond to typical questions.

CHAPTER TWELVE

Writing Online

'First we thought the PC was a calculator. Then we found out how to turn numbers into letters with ASCII – and we thought it was a typewriter. Then we discovered graphics, and we thought it was a television. With the World Wide Web, we've realised it's a brochure.'

Douglas Adams

The traditional book will be with us for some time yet; in spite of tough times in the industry it's holding up pretty well. And in the UK we publish a vast number of books per head of population. The United Nations Educational, Scientific and Cultural Organization (UNESCO) monitors both the number and types of books published per country per year, and reports that new titles in the UK increased by 28 per cent in 2005–6. The UK is among the top three publishers of books in the world, rivalled only by the US and China. The latest available figures from UNESCO at the time of writing put the US at the top of the list with 275,232 (2008); the UK second with 206,000 (2005); and China third with 136,226 (2007). According to Google Books, there are just under 130 million titles in the world.

However, there is no room for complacency – or Luddism. Douglas Adams was right: personal computing is changing so fast that we have to keep adjusting our expectations of what it can do. (Adams sadly died in 2001. Since his death the Internet has revolutionised the way we communicate. It is not just a brochure: it is a global conversation.) And personal computing is just one aspect of the huge changes that are affecting the conventional publishing model. The implosion of global book retailers like Borders must have profound implications for the industry. And print is not the only way to get your work out there. Think of the Internet as an addition to traditional publishing, and try to get as much as you can out of it. Its potential is vast, and, as a writer with a career to build and sustain, you would be foolish to ignore this.

But the sheer scale of the Web is daunting in itself, and its functions and social impact are changing all the time. According to the website Internet World Stats (www.Internetworldstats. com/stats.htm), in early 2011, 1,966,514,816 people across the planet were using the Internet: this is 28.7 per cent of the world's population. As I write, the proprietor of WikiLeaks Julian Assange is being accused of espionage by the US government; Facebook is endemic among teenagers – and used by an increasing number of adults – and Twitter is attracting both ordinary citizens and self-preoccupied celebrities in droves. At the end of 2010, Twitter had more than 165 million registered users, according to its blog. Inevitably, by the time you read this chapter, the virtual landscape will have shifted. But one thing is certain: it will still give you the chance to communicate with a huge number of potential readers.

The word 'communicate' is important here. One mistake that many authors make is to see the Internet as a shop window for their wares and nothing more. While this is important, what's really new about the Web is the opportunity it gives you to learn about your readers and potential readers – and to engage with them. Equally, at a time when conventional publishing is facing the double whammy of world recession and the rumoured 'death of the book', the

Internet gives you the chance to find existing communities of readers who share your interests. Linking with such groups can make the difference between your blog and website being lost in the Internet ether, and making them a hub of activity, buzzing with news and creative feedback. This is particularly applicable to niche genres like sci-fi and fantasy. Readers of these genres are likely to be IT-literate and to join social networking and fan sites and other online communities.

American entrepreneur and author Seth Godin sees the Internet as a tribal phenomenon, made up of a series of interest groups whom you can influence if you can engage them with your views. Godin's book *Tribes* looks at the phenomenon of the modern, global 'tribe', and explains how to develop and sustain links to the tribe that is relevant to you, using tools like Twitter, Facebook and blogging. As an author, of course, you will find that your tribe is your readers.

Setting this up will take time, at least initially, and cost money if you decide to hire someone to design your website. But you don't need to be a computer nerd. The key to success is to get organised, research your genre, know the market and be clear about what you want to do. Once you have done the groundwork, you can set up an author website and a blog. After that, you simply need to set aside a specific amount of time for your Web-related activities: you don't need to spend very long on this.

Author Websites

As a starting point, think about your readers and potential readers. If you are writing nonfiction, then the subject is likely to come first. Your goal should be to attract readers/ visitors who share your passion for your subject. To win their respect, you'll need to show that you are knowledgeable, reliable and up to date with current trends. If you are seen as an expert in your field, you will gradually build up traffic to your site – as long as you also develop your search-engine optimisation (SEO), which I will look at later. If you write a succession of books that relate to the same topic, this is a straightforward way to build up a fan base for your work.

On the other hand, if you write fiction your readers are likely to be more curious about you as an individual, so they will want to find out about you from your site. But this doesn't mean you need to display all your personal holiday snaps. Think carefully about how much you want to reveal about your private life. The Web enables you to establish a writing persona that is distinct from your actual identity. Show that you are a fan of other writers in your field, comment on their work, review relevant books and give your site as much personality and originality as you can. Think of your site as the equivalent of a teenager's bedroom, where your passions and interests are on display – but with a strategic intent.

The sophistication or otherwise of your website depends on your personal taste, and on your budget. You can build something very simple yourself. There is no need to be a technical wizard to do this: all you really need is a domain name and a Web host. Try sites like Build Your Own Website (www.build-your-website.co.uk) or BBC Webwise (www.bbc.co.uk/webwise/guides/building-websites). If you decide to hire a designer, make sure you choose someone who has experience of designing author sites, and who makes the site as flexible and interactive as possible, as well as making it visually appealing and easy to navigate. Web designers who work specifically with writers include Word Pool (www.wordpooldesign.co.uk) and Book Webs (www.bookwebs.co.uk). You may also – if you are lucky – find that your publisher will set up a site for you. But don't depend on this. Whatever style you go for, anyone who comes to your site will be looking for good content. They will want to be entertained as well as informed.

Don't assume that you can just set up a site and then just wait for readers to visit it – this is a dynamic medium, and the more than you add to the site and comment, the more accessible and enticing it will be. This means that you need to add to it, update it and expand it regularly and often.

One simple way of making your site dynamic is to give visitors access to your blog – more details on this in the next section. If you decide to build your own, a great resource is a self-published guide called *Plug Your Book: Online Marketing for Authors* by Steve Weber (Weber Books).

Do look at author sites before your start. See how they are designed, and how they reflect the style and personality of the author both visually and in terms of content. Linking to other sites and commenting on their posts is the simplest way of establishing your presence on the Internet, and making relevant online contacts.

I have listed some interesting sites below, belonging to both famous and lesser-known writers. They vary in style, sophistication and content, but all of them are an effective showcase for the author.

Ros Barber: www.rosbarber.com

Barber is a Brighton-based poet and academic who has been studying the life of Marlowe. Her site is an example of what can be done relatively simply.

Cory Doctorow: http://craphound.com

Doctorow is a Canadian blogger, journalist, and science-fiction author who co-edits the blog *Boing Boing*. He is in favour of liberalising copyright laws and supports the Creative Commons organisation, which promotes the sharing of creative work. His site is visually interesting and gives a flavour of Doctorow's style as well as his work.

Jasper Fforde: www.jasperfforde.com

Fforde's first novel, *The Eyre Affair*, was published in 2001, having being rejected by seventy-six publishers. It went on to be a cult best-seller. He is best known for his *Thursday Next* novels, and has begun another series of books entitled *Shades of Grey*. The site links to his blog, and demonstrates his interest in the Web. This is one of the best sites around, often updated, imaginative, witty, interactive and definitely one to look at before you set up your own.

Neil Gaiman: www.neilgaiman.co.uk

Gaiman is a prolific and high-profile author specialising in science fiction and fantasy, and has won a number of awards, including the Carnegie Medal. He is best known for his graphic-novel series *The Sandman* and other novels including *Stardust* and *The Graveyard Book*. This site is well designed and easy to negotiate and links to his blog. Gaiman has a million followers on Twitter and has established a virtual community of readers.

Scarlett Thomas: www.scarlettthomas.co.uk

Thomas has written eight novels, including *The End of Mr. Y* and *PopCo*, and teaches English literature at the University of Kent. This is a stylish site, which is easy on the eye and reflects Thomas's cultish, niche status as a writer.

Joanna Trollope: www.joannatrollope.com

Trollope is still one of the best-known women writers in the UK, and the author of a number of best-selling novels including *The Rector's Wife* and *Marrying the Mistress*. Her site is all-singing, all-dancing and has a huge amount of information about her various works of fiction. Her podcasts are dauntingly professional, but we can all learn.

Jeanette Winterson: www.jeanettewinterson.com

Winterson's first novel, *Oranges Are Not the Only Fruit*, won the 1985 Whitbread Prize for a First Novel, and the TV adaptation later won a BAFTA for Best Drama. She has also written numerous other novels for both adults and children. This is an excellent site, again giving a good insight into Winterson's life and interests as well as information about her books for both adults and children, and a link to her chatty blog.

Author websites

Tips from The Urban Muse
(at www.urbanmusewriter.com)

Susan Johnston (a.k.a. The Urban Muse), a freelance writer, copy editor and blogger, based in Boston, Massachusetts, comments on author blogs.

> **Testimonials build credibility.** A lot of writers had testimonials on their websites, and a lot didn't. If you're in the latter camp, then you're missing out on an easy marketing opportunity. Not sure how to get testimonials? Just ask your repeat clients or editors the next time you finish a project. Most will be happy to oblige.

> **Bad site navigation makes a bad impression.** Make it easy on editors, clients, and readers by including site navigation (home, bio, news, etc.) on every single page and in a place that's obvious. One (professionally designed and otherwise gorgeous) website had the navigation buried at the bottom, so I had to scroll down to find it. A few

continued

---

self-made sites were either missing links back to the homepage or had links that didn't work. And by the way, underlining text that isn't hyperlinked is a big tease.

An approachable, personable photo adds personality. Headshots are not mandatory for writers, but a good one can give editors and clients a sense of who you are and what you're like. No one expects you to be a glamour girl (unless your niche is beauty), so choose a photo that is flattering but actually looks like you. A candid photo can work if it's not too blurry. If you'd rather not include a photo, then that's fine, too. Some writers choose to use a funny childhood photo, a cartoon, stock images, or magazine covers instead or in addition to a traditional headshot.

Huge headers detract from your content. Yes, it is nice to have a jumbo-sized graphic of a typewriter or a globe or butterflies or rainbows, but it it takes up so much of the screen that you can't see anything else, that is a problem. The most important information should be 'above the fold' so that the reader doesn't have to scroll to figure out your specialties or credentials. Plus, big beautiful graphics take more time to load and you don't want people to get impatient and leave your site, do you?

Blogging

Blogs are simple websites with an interactive element. Setting up a blog is easy, and updating the content and posting is like writing an online diary. The most challenging and time-consuming aspect of running a professional blog is making sure that you get traffic and that you attract comment from visitors. And potential visitors are out there – 77 per cent of frequent Internet users regularly access blogs.

Once you have set up a blog, don't just post comments. Exploit its interactive capacity. There is not much point in blogging unless you can create a sense of community and dialogue with your readers. When you are establishing yourself online, it's particularly important to visit other blogs and sites, familiarising yourself with what other writers are doing online, and taking part in the cyber conversation that relates to your work by commenting on other blog posts. The best blogs aren't monologues: they are a conversation, full of ideas, opinions and inspirations, and give people with similar interests the chance to share links to useful Web content, news and so on. Do also look at blogs that don't work so well. As with novels, it's easier to see the join when you look at something that falls short, whereas a brilliant piece of work can be inspirational but harder to analyse.

Blog regularly and often – at least once a week – and make your posts lively and interesting. There are plenty of blogs that feature the mind-numbingly boring activities of interchangeable families, illustrated with endless photos of their guinea pig/novelty birthday cake/new garden shed. This is not the way for a writer to go. (If you really want to have that kind of blog, feel free, but set up a different one for your writing activities and leave the guinea pig out of it.)

The great advantage of a blog is that you don't have to spend long writing. Your regular, topical posts will encourage potential readers to come back time and again, and you will thus increase potential sales of your next book. (If you are self-published, you can sell your work directly from your website, so do make sure that your blog and your site are connected. And whether you are self-published or contracted to a publisher, you can use your blog to test out ideas, and see what sort of reception they get from your readers.) Blogs also rank highly in search-engine results, so they are easy to find – you have a good chance of reaching people who have never heard of you before this way.

Search-Engine Optimisation

To make sure this happens, as well as blogging regularly it's also essential to use as many 'key words' in your copy as you can. These are simply words that lots of people in the blogosphere are putting into Google or other search engines. You can see which words are most searched for by using the free Google Trends service (www.google.com/trends) and then make sure to use them in your posts. You need to stick at this for some time before you see the effects, but, if you blog regularly, highlight the key words and cover similar subjects, you will inevitably attract visitors to your site. Make sure the content is readable, lively, informative and relevant to their interests, and they are more likely to come back again. And, before you start, add relevant blogs that you like to your bookmarks (called 'favourites' in Internet Explorer).

To find a list of the most popular blogs, go to www.Technorati. com/pop/blogs. And you can also find blogs with relevant content by searching the following blogs by keyword:

- www.Blogsearch.Google.com
- www.Feedster.com
- www.IceRocket.com

When you have found some relevant blogs, look at the other blogs they are linking to – you are likely to find that several of these are worth adding to your list. To keep track of all your blogs use a newsreader or aggregator. This will gather any new posts for you and let you know when they appear. Useful sites that do this for free include www.Bloglines.com and Google Reader at www.google.com/reader.

Blog search engines such as Technorati (http://technorati. com) are used to search blog content. They provide current information on both popular searches and tags used to categorise blog postings. Find out what other bloggers are saying about your topics and stay up to date. You can also bookmark interesting blog posts using Technorati for future reference.

You can use widgets such as http://feedjit.com and Google analytics (www.google.com/analytics) to find out which of your blog posts readers are most interested in – and how well search-engine-optimised your blog is. Google Trends, which I mentioned earlier, is also useful for this. Asking other bloggers to link to you and list you in their links will give you 'actuality' with search engines, so you rank higher in the search results.

Top 10 tips for search engine optimisation

- Update often and Google will find you.
- Headlines should begin with the keyword if possible.
- Ask other bloggers to link to you and to list you in their links.
- Get linked to relevant high-ranked sites and blogs.
- Use keywords in your headline and in your copy.
- Link your blog to all your social-media accounts.
- Link back to your previous posts.
- Comment on other blogs on similar topics to your own.
- Put links back to your blog whenever you comment on other people's.
- Provide links to useful external stuff in your posts.

Blogging and the Law

Blogging is subject to the laws of libel, though this may surprise you given some of the outrageous content that you will see online. Remember that, while a defamatory statement is not actionable unless it is published, as a blogger you are automatically the publisher of your work as well as its author. Blogging is a form of publishing. You can libel someone by writing about them on a personal blog, provided at least one person accesses the defamatory material. Prosecutions are rare, partly because newspapers and broadcasters are an easier target than the huge number of bloggers who post comment every day. And it's true that celebrities – and indeed private individuals – have little power to suppress confidential information about their lives once it goes up on the Web. But the free-for-all nature of online information does not give you *carte blanche* to publish anything your like – the WikiLeaks controversy is proof of that.

The US pressure group Reporters without Borders (http://en.rsf.org) has branches throughout the world, and estimates that currently two hundred bloggers and reporters are behind bars. The rule is to put on your blog only what you would put in your books. Be as bold as you like, but be clear about potential consequences.

Social Networking

As of January 2011, Facebook had more than 600 million worldwide users (250 million of them accessing the site via mobile devices), while Twitter statistics from September 2010 boasted 175 million users (by the time you read this, these figures will no doubt be hopelessly out of date, such is the growth of these two Internet phenomena). Facebook recently announced that it has over 400 million worldwide users, while Twitter has 75 million, who collectively 'tweet' 50 million times a day. Tweeting is popular with celebrities like Stephen Fry, and other well-known writers on Twitter include Margaret Atwood, Meg Cabot, Daisy Goodwin, Alice Hoffman and Chuck Palahniuk. Both of these forms of online communication are useful for talking to other writers, making new contacts and developing and sustaining a group of potential readers.

While Facebook is useful as a tool to communicate with people you know, and to put you in touch with people *they* know, Twitter connects you with strangers, which means that you can develop your network of useful contacts much more quickly. The key to using Twitter successfully as a writer is to get a group of followers who like your writing, and who will spread the word about you, particularly when you have a new book to promote. As a writer, you also have an advantage: writers are popular on Twitter, and your pithy, succinct opinions will be more interesting than those of many airhead celebrities. It is also a good way of honing your Hemingway-esque style. You can't waffle on Twitter, because everything has to be said in 140 characters or fewer.

Interviewed in the February 2011 issue of *Writing Magazine*, Bethanne Patrick, who tweets as 'Bookmaven' and has around 30,000 followers on Twitter, comments,

In today's publishing climate, having a platform is quite important. 'Platform' means you already have some kind of audience and credentials. Whether you're a celebrity, a crafter or a social worker, if you want to publish a book, take a close look at what you have to offer. Do you have a blog? Do you give talks or lectures? Have you already published articles? Twitter can give you a platform – or at least a few planks of one!

Anthony Levings, of academic publishing house Gylphi Publishing, makes another useful point in the same article, suggesting that each online element of the platform should be broken down into the different roles they serve:

For example, a website should advertise and inform visitors about your publications, associated news and upcoming events; a blog should be for fans of your writing, or those looking for a more personal view of what you are about, and a Twitter/Facebook presence should be seen as an informal opportunity for integrating yourself into a wider community.

But all of this takes time and the Internet can be a serious distraction. If you are trying to get into your writing 'zone', there is nothing worse than checking your email or Twitter account every five minutes. And it has the effect of eroding your attention span, as well as eating into your thinking time. Novelist Yiyun Li deliberately rationed her use of the Web so that she could get more reading done. 'As a mother of two young children who teaches full time and writes books, I don't have much time for reading. I decided to give up web-surfing to stay a better, calmer bookworm,' she wrote in the *New Statesman*.

Since disconnecting herself, she has read works by Homer, Montaigne, Shakespeare, Tolstoy, Dostoevsky, Turgenev and Dickens. Her reading list may sound daunting, but time spent online is also time spent away from writing. Keeping focused on your work is particularly challenging if you write on your laptop or PC and are constantly thinking about tweeting or checking your Facebook wall. In the immortal words of Danny in *Withnail and I*, you need to 'find your neutral space' – and the Internet is not that space.

As with all aspects of an author's long-term career, the solution is to find the right balance. The best approach is to get out there as much as possible and build your profile, so that you can show that people are interested in you and what you have to say. Internet presence is becoming an important factor, which publishers take into account when deciding whether to take on new projects. But make sure you use the Internet in a focused, professional way. I too have shopped for vintage tat on eBay, looked at celebrity cellulite on the *Daily Mail* site and Googled everyone I knew in 1986, so I know how easy it is to be distracted.

Publishers Online

Publishers are becoming increasingly aware of ways to exploit the power of the Internet, and are aware that the rise of the e-book will have a significant impact on the nature of the market. Several publishers have set up their own websites, and these are worth checking out. I have highlighted a few examples below, but this is not an exhaustive list and you'll need to do your own searches. (A Twitter account can help with this, particularly if you follow a number of publishers.)

Penguin

We Tell Stories (http://wetellstories.co.uk)

Penguin has set up this digital writing project to experiment with new forms of storytelling that put the Internet to creative use. Authors involved in the experiment include Booker-shortlisted Mohsin Hamid, teen-fiction author Kevin Brooks, Naomi Alderman and thriller writer Nicci French (husband-and-wife duo Nicci Gerrard and Sean French.) The stories vary in quality – my vote is for Nicci French – but it's worth checking out to get some ideas and see what's current.

HarperCollins

Authonomy (www.authonomy.com)

Authonomy was set up in 2008 'to flush out the brightest, freshest new literature around' and is a showcase for the unpublished, self-published or anyone wanting to attract attention to their work. It's essentially a social networking site on which budding authors post their work. Other writers and readers review and rank their efforts, the most popular of which get feedback from HarperCollins editors, and may go forward for possible publication.

Canongate

Meet at the Gate (www.meetatthegate.com)

Independent Scottish publisher Canongate has developed a strong reputation and is one of the most highly respected small publishers in the UK. Writers on its books include Michel Faber and Yann Martell. Its stated aim is 'to publish new talent from around the world, whilst retaining the essence of the Scottish Canon'. Canongate's website Meet at the Gate is a genuine forum for discussion and debate. The site acts as a 'cultural hub', which is independent of Canongate itself and which encourages visitors to contribute their own personal recommendations, passions and opinions.

Print/Online Publications

The literary magazine used to play a significant part in the life of a budding author, publishing articles, short stories, novel extracts and poetry. Many have now sadly disappeared, but there are signs that the Internet is making it possible for small magazines to survive. They are both a useful way of reading cutting-edge work and a potential outlet for your own. Here are some examples:

Notes from the Underground
(www.notesfromtheunderground.co.uk)

Free literary and arts-based magazine that aims 'to provide the very best in contemporary fiction, cartoons, poems and non-fiction features' and is a platform for new and emerging writers.

The view from here (www.viewfromheremagazine.com)

Print and online literary magazine that aims 'to add new and lasting literary merit to the body of English writing by championing and encouraging the best emerging and developing writers and poets and by creating an appetite in readers for quality literature'. The magazine comes out in both digital and printed format and carries articles from the likes of literary agent Simon Trewin and Scott Pack from The Friday Project.

3 AM (www.3ammagazine.com)

'Edgy' literary website that has a devoted following among fans of offbeat, obscure, experimental and other niche writing genres. Aimed at writers whose work breaks boundaries and taboos.

For Books' Sake (http://forbookssake.net)

Specialises in women's fiction with an irreverent take on everyone from Jane Austen to Poppy Z. Brite. Covers events, news about small presses and lesser-known women writers and reviews of both fiction and nonfiction.

Traditional magazines like the *London Magazine* (www.thclondonmagazine.org) and Mslexia (www.mslexia.co.uk) also have websites as well as appearing in print form.

E-Books

Whether the rise of the e-book will make your future as a writer easier or more difficult is uncertain. Currently, no one knows what this future will look like. But it's possible that a new publishing model will emerge from the increasing popularity and availability of e-books. One theory is that 'the long tail' will help authors both create their work and find an audience. This is a retailing concept, which describes the strategy of selling a wide range of 'niche items' in small quantities as an alternative to selling a narrow range of popular items in large quantities. Potentially, this is an antidote to the mass-market mindset that dominates mainstream publishing at the moment. To find out more, read *The Long Tail: Why the Future of Business Is Selling Less of More* by Chris Anderson.

However, no one actually knows how this will work. And no one knows how to make significant profits from e-publishing. The most commonly used e-readers are the Amazon Kindle and Sony's PRS-500. In July 2010, Amazon reported that sales of Kindle outnumbered sales of hardback books. (Paperback sales are still higher than Kindle or hardbacks.) Stieg Larsson's *The Girl Who Played with Fire* is selling on Amazon for £2.70. And there are around 2 million free books available for download to an e-reader: all fiction published before 1900, for example.

What is certain is that e-books are currently making a significant impact on the market. *The Bookseller* reports that USA e-book sales have been tripling year on year, from 1 per cent of total sales in 2008 to 9 per cent in 2010. And, according to the newspaper and website *USA Today*, millions of Americans received iPads, Kindles and other digital reading devices as Christmas presents, leading to an unprecedented surge in sales of e-books. E-book versions of the top six books outsold the print versions in January 2011, and 19 of the books in the top 50 had higher e-book than print sales.

The UK appears to be following suit. According to research service Book Marketing Limited, although e-books accounted for just over 1 per cent of book purchases in the last three months of 2010, this share more than doubled in the first four weeks of 2011. This increase is taking place at a time when British consumers are buying fewer books – down from 344 million in 2008 to 339 million in 2010 – and the amount spent fell from £2,341 million to £2,183 million. Meanwhile, one-third of UK trade publishers reported in 2011 that over 10 per cent of their total book revenue would come from e-books by 2012, according to research released in spring 2011 by the company Publishing Technology.

The rise of the e-book also means that self-publishing has a new lease of life, as the success of sites such as www.lulu.com proves. The overheads on publishing a book online are negligible, and – as we have seen above – using social networking, blogging and Internet PR can help you market and sell your work.

Online Writing

It's also possible that the art of fiction writing itself will be changed by the Internet. These are early days, and my own view is that the change is likely to be limited, because fiction writers tend to work solo, find collaboration difficult and prefer to use the Internet as a tool that helps them to do their existing job more efficiently, rather than exploit its more revolutionary aspects. For instance, while scriptwriters use software like Final Draft to collaborate on a screenplay, even when they are working in different cities or different countries, there is no equivalent in terms of fiction writing. There are novel-writing packages that help with layout, but that's it.

The potential for change is there, however, and some writers are experimenting with new fiction-writing models. In 2009 US thriller writer James Patterson wrote an online thriller called *Airborne*. He wrote the first paragraph: 'The sky had turned grey as the four men walked nervously past the police car . . .' He then asked people to finish it – in 250 words or fewer. The writers of the best twenty-eight responses wrote the next twenty-eight chapters of the novel. Another innovator is Naomi Alderman, who has written an online story called 'The Winter House' (www.thewinterhouse.co.uk), which uses the form very creatively. iPhone novels have made some impact in Japan, and here in the UK four Brighton writers – Susanna Jones, Alison Macleod, Jeff Noon and William Shaw – have written the beginning of an online novel called *217 Babel Street* (www.217babel.com), which tells the story of a group of eccentric tenants in a weird apartment building.

Online novel-writing communities have also sprung up in both the UK and US. One example is www.thenoveltree.com. Contributors read what has been written, add to the story, and join online chats about how the narrative is developing. There are a number of different novels on the site. Another example is National Novel Writing Month (www.nanowrimo.org). Each year, proto-novelists sign up for this project on 1 November and write 60,000 words in 30 days, recording their progress on Nanowrimo's website.

The Internet is also the natural home of poetry and short fiction, which lend themselves to reading on screen and in bite-sized chunks more readily than longer narratives. You can post short stories on a number of sites. For example, take a look at Booksie (www.booksie.com). And the short, short form is also well served – check out sites that specialise in 'flash fiction' (stories of a thousand words or fewer) and micro fiction (http://microfictiononline.com).

Again, publishers are not entirely sure how to make the most of this flowering of online talent. One tactic is to publish online writing in book form. Examples include the anonymous blog of research scientist Dr Brooke Magnanti, *Belle de Jour: Diary of a London Call Girl*, which became the novel, *The Intimate Adventures of a London Call Girl*; and New Yorker Julie Powell's blog about spending a year cooking the recipes in Paris chef Julia Child's cookbook, which became a novel and later a film starring Meryl Streep.

Writing Online: The Lowdown

- The book is not dead yet – but you do need to be online as well as on paper. The potential of the Internet is vast.
- The Internet is not just a shop window for your wares: it is also a new way of communicating with readers.

- Find your 'tribe' – those who share your interests, potential readers and other writers. Use the Internet to develop your relationship with them.
- A website and a blog are useful to all authors and should ideally be part of your toolkit. They are part of your public platform.
- Social networking using Facebook and Twitter is another way in which you can boost your profile online. You can keep up to date by following writers/publishing experts on Twitter.
- Don't let your Internet presence distract you too much from the job in hand: writing regularly, and every day if possible.

CHAPTER THIRTEEN

The Public Writer

'I don't intend to simply go away and write my plays and be a good boy. I intend to remain an independent and political intelligence in my own right.'
                                                                    Harold Pinter

What is the pinnacle of a writing career? Fame? Money? Some writers achieve this – not many, but a few. An even smaller number achieve both of these things and something else too: public respect. They become establishment figures. They may even be offered titles and a seat in the House of Lords. We look to them in the expectation (sometimes misplaced) that they will tell us how to live. Naïvely, perhaps, we hope the years they have spent inventing stories have made them wise.

This is a career stage that survives death: Jane Austen, Charles Dickens, George Eliot and William Shakespeare seem to offer us a moral compass when politicians and conventional religion let us down. However, there are some living writers who are also afforded this respect: Martin Amis, Margaret Atwood and Salman Rushdie are all public commentators as well as successful artists. Both the depth and the reach of their work gives them a perceived right to comment on world events. Seeing these writers as role models in the belief that you may be equally famous one day is a bit like hoping that a lottery win will sort out your interest-only mortgage. Nevertheless, we may be able to learn from their example.

Let's start with the position of Poet Laureate, or official public poet. In many ways, this august title is actually the closest thing we have to a modern court jester, though humour is now an optional extra. And it's a tradition that goes back to the seventeenth century, when Ben Jonson was appointed by James I in 1617. Some of the greatest English poets have followed in Jonson's footsteps, including John Dryden and Alfred Tennyson. But this public and official role does not appeal to all poets: John Gray, Walter Scott and Philip Larkin all turned the position down.

When Philip Larkin made it plain he didn't want to be Poet Laureate in 1984, Ted Hughes was next in line. This might at first seem like an unlikely choice. Employing the brooding, saturnine Yorkshireman to write verses to mark official occasions like the Queen Mum's birthday looked a bit like hiring Heathcliff to hand out balloons. But Hughes customised the role, and used it as a way to put his views – which were anything but 'establishment' in the conventional sense – onto the public stage. His public poems may not have been his finest in artistic terms, but they formed part of his campaign for the imagination and against what he saw as our spiritually bankrupt social values. At the end of Hughes's obituary in the *Independent* in 1998, Lachlan Mackinnon wrote, 'When time has winnowed the harvest of an extraordinarily productive career, a substantial body of very remarkable verse will be left. Ted Hughes wrote great poems in a time which cared little either for greatness or for poetry. So doing, he conferred dignity on the Laureateship which was rightly his.'

Carol Ann Duffy was appointed Poet Laureate in 2009. Not only was she the first woman to take up the post, she is also a lesbian, and is fiercely protective of her private life. On her appointment, she announced that she would donate her yearly stipend of £5,750 to the Poetry Society to fund a new poetry prize for the best annual collection. 'I didn't want to take on what basically is an honour on behalf of other poets and complicate it with money,' she told the *Guardian*. 'I thought it was better to give it back to poetry.' Duffy has written on a wide range of public issues, including an injury to David Beckham and a fatal tram crash in the TV soap *Coronation Street*. Like Hughes, she has made the Laureateship her own, celebrating and commemorating landmarks in popular culture as well as royal events.

Writers and the Public Stage

In many parts of the world, poets and novelists become intellectual leaders, and it's also more acceptable for writers to enter political life than it is in the UK. Václav Havel was president of the Czech Republic from 1989 to 2003; Michael Ignatieff was leader of the opposition in Canada from 2008 to 2011 and Mario Vargas Llosa ran for the presidency of Peru in 1990. Arguably, any serious writer is concerned with the great social issues of the day – though the writers on the Man Booker shortlist are often accused of not being.

Whether you see yourself as public writer or not is a matter of personal choice. Perhaps you see your work solely as entertainment, and want to develop your career in those terms. But it does no harm to see your ambitions in a wider context. It's empowering and inspiring to think that you can write not just to entertain but also to explain. Graham Greene described some of his books as 'entertainments', the implication being that he meant novels such as *The Power and the Glory* and *The End of the Affair* to do much more than fill an idle hour. Most serious writers believe it's their responsibility to engage with moral issues. In his book *Modern Man in Search of a Soul*, the psychologist Carl Jung said that the poet's work should meet the spiritual needs of his society. In that sense, every writer is a poet.

Giving Something Back

There's also an honourable tradition of writers engaging directly with charitable and voluntary work. J. K. Rowling is well known for giving large sums to charity, for instance. She donated the handwritten history of the family of her character Sirius Black to Book Aid International, supports other charities including the single-parent families' support group Gingerbread (itself formally called One Parent Families) and co-founded the Children's High Level Group, which wants to see UN minimum standards for the care of children implemented in Europe and beyond. Another famous writer with charitable leanings is Nick Hornby, who jointly set up the Tree House Trust in 1997 to provide an educational centre of excellence for children with autism, and has recently launched the Ministry of Stories with the Arts Council. This is a new story writing venture which aims to inspire a 'nation of storytellers'.

Issues associated with freedom of speech and thought as well as social justice have engaged writers like Martin Amis. Amis spoke out dramatically after the 9/11 attacks, writing in the *Guardian* about 'species fear', which caught the mood of the time if not the exact nature of the threat from Islamic fundamentalism. In 1987 he also produced *Einstein's Monsters*, a collection of five stories on the theme of nuclear weapons. This begins with a long essay entitled 'Thinkability' in which he wrote, 'Nuclear weapons repel all thought, perhaps because they can end all thought.' In 2002 he wrote *Koba the Dread: Laughter and the Twenty Million*, which attacked the attitude of many Western intellectuals towards the atrocities of Lenin and Stalin.

Meanwhile, Margaret Atwood is committed to her environmental campaign work and is a prominent member of the Green Party in Canada, and her book *The Year of the Flood*, a sequel to *Oryx and Crake*, is about environmental catastrophe. And, most notoriously of all, the global controversy that followed the publication of Salman Rushdie's *The Satanic Verses* in 1988 shows just how seriously the written word is still taken. Rushdie's book influenced the zeitgeist as well as reflecting it, and made him a very public writer indeed. The death fatwa imposed on him by Ayatollah Ruhollah Khomeini of Iran also put the issue of free speech centre stage, and forced many people in the West to clarify their position. Free speech at all costs? Or only when it doesn't clash with vociferous religious extremism? Without *The Satanic Verses*, it would have been easier to be complacent about the subject.

Becoming a Public Writer

Social concerns have inspired the work of some our best-loved authors. For instance, George Orwell said his ambition was to 'make political writing into an art'. In his 1946 essay 'Why I Write' he wrote, 'Every line of serious work that I have written since 1936 has been written, directly or indirectly, against Totalitarianism and for Democratic Socialism, as I understand it.' His inventions of terms like 'Newspeak', 'double-think' and 'Big Brother' have influenced the language and the way that we think, and his insistence that language should be clear, precise and uncluttered was not just an aesthetic judgement, but a political one.

In a world in which consumerism, greed, myopia and political passivity are the norm, there are plenty of targets for writers, and plenty of causes to support. If we don't take any interest in the issues of the day, then we are implicitly accepting that our books are just products that we want to sell. Writing to be read is in itself a communal act, and being a public writer is something that is open to all of us, not just a perk for those who are already part of the Establishment.

Subjects that naturally concern writers include literacy, education and freedom of speech. An increasing number are following Atwood's example and supporting environmental campaign work. Many support PEN (www.internationalpen.org.uk), the international organisation that works to promote literature and human rights. International PEN is a membership association with 144 branches in more than one hundred countries, and English PEN is a founder member of the parent body. It runs a committee that organises Writers in Prison committees, working on behalf of persecuted writers around the world, and campaigns to improve the understanding of freedom of expression as a fundamental human right.

Past presidents include John Galsworthy, H. G. Wells, Rosamond Lehmann, Stephen Spender and Lady Antonia Fraser. And one of the most famous and active members of PEN was the late Harold Pinter, who saw political engagement as intrinsic to his writing and was a vocal critic of US foreign policy. But any writer can support PEN's work, by supporting writers in prison, joining their campaigns for free speech and becoming a member of the organisation. (See box for details about PEN and its campaigning work.)

Becoming a public writer – useful organisations

You don't have to wait till you are famous to put something back into society. Here is a list of organisations that are happy to hear from writers or anyone interested in books and literacy.

The Ministry of Stories (www.ministryofstories.org)

The Ministry of Stories is based in Hoxton, east London, and is a community project that aims to help children and teenagers to develop their writing and literacy skills. More than two hundred volunteer writers, artists and teachers provide students with free workshops and mentoring sessions. The project was founded by author Nick Hornby with Arts Council backing, and is inspired by author Dave Eggers's 826 Valencia literary movement in America, which is a nonprofit tutoring, writing, and publishing organisation that helps school students from six to eighteen with their writing skills, and offers additional support to teachers 'to get their classes excited about writing'.

High-profile writers involved in the Ministry of Stories scheme include Roddy Doyle, Zadie Smith, Meera Syal and former Children's Laureate Michael Morpurgo. There are plans to extend the project across the country, and the organisation is looking for volunteers. You can apply to be a volunteer mentor through its website, and training is provided.

Volunteer Reading Help (www.vrh.org.uk)

Volunteer Reading Help (VRH) is a national charity that helps children who struggle with their reading to develop a love of reading and learning. VRH recruits and trains reading helpers to work with children aged from six to eleven who find reading a challenge and may need extra support and mentoring. Volunteers join a network of trained reading helpers and support the same children week in, week out, giving each an hour of intensive, one-to-one time. VRH works both in schools and outside the classroom, and also works with children in the care system, who are often the most vulnerable children in society.

Writers in Prison Network
(www.writersinprisonnetwork.org)

The Writers in Prison Network was appointed by the Arts Council in 1998 to administer the Writers in Residence in Prison Scheme, which was set up in 1992 by the Arts Council and the Home Office. This is an educational charity that offers a range of distance learning courses to prisoners. The scheme employs

continued

writers who are experienced or established in particular literary fields. Many have been creative-writing tutors, or have worked in publishing, the theatre, television, radio or journalism. In 2010–11 there were 16 writers' residencies in prisons (plus a number of affiliated residencies and development projects) and four new resident writers were appointed.

Writers in Residence

A writer-in-residence is normally a published writer who is based within an organisation or institution for a set period of time. Writers will divide their time between working with the 'host' community and working on their own writing. Organisations that have taken part in this scheme include hospitals, schools, libraries, museums and universities.

The aim is to develop writing projects and activities, improve literacy skills, encourage creativity and mentor new writers. Often, the writer will also help the organisation to develop a body of work which reflects its culture and history. This might take the form of an anthology of new writing produced by the people who work there. In addition, the residency also gives them the chance to develop their own work and draw inspiration from the place where they are working.

In 2009, the writer and presenter Alain de Botton became the first ever writer-in-residence at a UK airport. He spent a week in Heathrow's Terminal Five, where he was given access to all areas, and researched a book about the experience. According to de Botton, airports encapsulate the modern world, featuring 'interconnection, fast travel, the destruction of nature . . . dreams of consumerism and travel'. Residencies are also changing – with 'virtual writing residencies' now coming into being. A recent virtual residency in Dumfries and Galloway in Scotland was set up to provide online writing projects, coordinated by the writer-in-residence Jules Horne, a fiction writer and playwright.

Writers' Fellowships

The Royal Literary Fund's Fellowship scheme for writers was launched in 1999 and is based in UK universities and colleges of higher education. RLF Fellows are established professional writers 'of literary merit' who represent a wide range of genres, including biography, translation and scientific writing. In its first ten years, the network of posts involved departments of science and technology as well as the humanities.

The Fellowship has been designed for published writers with at least two (sole-authored) books of any genre already published (or, for playwrights or screenwriters, mainstream theatre works produced or scripts broadcast). Applicants must also be English speakers and citizens of the UK, the European Union or a Commonwealth country. You can apply if you are a citizen of another country if you have been living in the UK for at least three years. The selection process is a competitive one. Once you apply, your literary merit and suitability for the scheme will be measured against those of other candidates in that round – this is not an easy option!

The RLF Fellowship scheme has expanded since it was set up, and currently some 90 writers are working in 67 universities. In the longer term, it hopes to work in more institutions of higher education. In 2011 it was anticipating that there would be forty vacancies in 2012 and a similar number in 2013.

Going Local

So where do you start? It would not be a good idea to offer your services as a Man Booker judge if you are unpublished and unheard of, or to apply for a Royal Literary Fellowship if you don't fulfil the criteria they set out. But being a public writer is not only about playing a part on the national stage. You can be part of your local community by offering to talk about writing or run workshops in local schools, by supporting local literacy initiatives (contact Volunteer Reading Help to find out what is happening in your area) and even by working in your local charity bookshops, which will put you in touch with both those who are interested in the good cause you are working for and people who care about books and reading. Looking at your local area and assessing its potential in terms of what you can contribute will help your morale, and your focus, and will inevitably bring you into contact with people who are useful to you in the quest to promote your own work.

As with so many aspects of running a writing career, your activities will not fit into neat categories, and your efforts to promote your work and your community involvement will overlap. With this in mind, if there are no readings or open-mic sessions going on in your local library or in pubs or cafés in your area, you could set something up. It needn't be weekly or even monthly, and, while it will take up time, you will be forging useful links. An annual event, linking to existing literary talks or festivals, might put your town or city on the map, and create a real buzz of excitement about your local creative-writing scene.

The Public Writer: The Lowdown

- A minority of successful writers become public figures, whose opinions are respected.
- Public roles such as Poet Laureate are available to such writers, though not all authors feel comfortable working in an 'official' capacity.
- There is also an honourable tradition of writers who do charitable work: both J. K. Rowling and Nick Hornby are committed to a number of good causes.
- Well-known authors like Martin Amis and Salman Rushdie are also celebrated champions of free speech.
- But writing is a communal act, and becoming a public writer is open to all of us, not just the famous few.

• If you want to put your writing to good use, you can support organisations like PEN and the Writer in Prison Network, or get in touch with relevant groups working in your local area.

CHAPTER FOURTEEN

Grants and Prizes

'How many writers toil away for years and for nothing? How many good books vanish without a trace? Too, too many not to make the whole endeavour seem foolish and soul-killing. It happens that the silence that surrounds the writer becomes permanent, engulfs the writer forever. And sometimes, when the writer has not only talent but luck, the silence is broken by a great deal of noise.'

Yann Martel on winning the 2002 Man Booker Prize

Of course, we all want to be award-winning. We all want to win the Nobel Prize in Literature, if we are honest, even if our fiction focuses exclusively on the antics of a herd of ditsy housewives who are slightly bored with their husbands. Literary prizes are set up for all sorts of reasons. Some, like the Betty Trask, are set up to honour the memory of a writer. Others are set up by public bodies or literary magazines with the dual aim of recognising new fiction and attracting some publicity to the organisers. And the most generous prizes have been set up in order to add lustre – and a hint of culture – to corporate names. Writers benefit, of course, but don't get the competition business out of proportion. In some ways, it is all a game. The most successful, award-garlanded writers in our culture are not necessarily those who are the most original or imaginative. Many brilliant authors who have written equally brilliant novels have never had a sniff of Man Booker glory.

Ultimately, beyond a certain level of competence, opinions about the merit of this writer or that one are a matter of subjective opinion. (I know that this very opinion is itself a matter of subjective opinion, but let's move on.) Awards don't go to the very best writers, necessarily, but they do showcase the work of those who have something to contribute to the contemporary scene. Fiction, like any other aspect of cultural life, is subject to fads and fashion. Awards help readers to make a choice, and in the current publishing environment this is of even more importance to a new or little-known writer than it was when the Booker was first awarded in 1969. (It was the Booker-McConnell Prize, but soon became known simply as the Booker Prize. 'Man' was added when the Man Group began to sponsor the prize in 2002.) Even established writers find that winning the Man Booker can transform their fortunes. It's a tricky balance to find, but, ideally, as a writer you should be aware of the awards system and be well informed about it while maintaining a healthy scepticism about its relevance to your work. Winning an award will increase your profile as an author, and you'll have free publicity and access to new readers. So, whatever the reason for their existence, you should try to win awards, and make sure that you know what prizes you are eligible for. Don't expect your agent or your publisher to find out for you – in this, as in so many areas of your publishing life, you need to take the initiative.

Being award-winning can certainly make an enormous difference to your status, and your sales. Naomi Alderman, author of *Disobedience* (Viking) experienced this when she won the Orange First Book award in 2005. 'Winning a high-profile prize always has an effect on a writer's career: it guarantees you a certain amount of review coverage, and ensures that publishers will be interested in your next work,' she says.

Writing in *Mslexia*, Kate Mosse, co-founder of the Orange Prize for Fiction, points out that prizes make headlines, commenting, 'The indisputable fact is, whether you love prizes or hate them, they remain an effective way of promoting the arts.'

The Power of Prizes

Together with word-of-mouth recommendations and good reviews, a literary prize may turn an obscure book into a cultural event. Getting onto a high-profile shortlist can have a seismic effect on the prospects for a book that has been published by a small house. In 2010 the Costa shortlist attracted public attention to a number of books of this kind. The First Novel Award category for the prize, which was for the 'most enjoyable' books published between 1 November 2009 and 31 October 2010, included Kishwar Desai's *Witness the Night* (Beautiful Books), Nikesh Shukla's *Coconut Unlimited* (Quartet Books) and Simon Thirsk's *Not Quite White* (Gomer Press).

New awards like the People's Book Prize, organised by Delancey Press, are another way for a new or little-known author to reach more readers. The People's Book Prize is voted for entirely by the public, and this year most of the prizewinners were unknown writers published by small, independent companies.

Book Promotions

Remember that being selected for a promotion can be another form of 'prize'. Not the three-for-two promotions in high street bookshops, which publishers have to pay for, but a recommendation from Richard Madeley and Judy Finnigan. In spite of the fact that their TV show *Richard & Judy* is no more, an *R&J* sticker can still help raise your profile, and shift copies of your book. In 2010, this promotion was running in more than one thousand W. H. Smith stores.

What's more, it's not necessarily the most literary prizes that earn you the highest public profile. More people are aware of the *Richard & Judy* 'Book Club' segment than the Nobel Prize in Literature or the Man Booker Prize, a *Bookseller* survey has found. More than 50 per cent of respondents said they had heard of *Richard & Judy*, while only 47 per cent had heard of the Nobel (but see 'The history of fiction prizes' below) and only 43 per cent were familiar with the Man Booker.

Not that the Man Booker is to be sniffed at, of course. Even a well-established author like Howard Jacobson has found that winning has added a new lustre to his career. (Some think Jacobson has been overlooked by the literary establishment because he has committed the sin of being amusing.) The day after the announcement of his Man Booker prize win with *The Finkler Question* (Bloomsbury) his publisher announced that it would be printing another 50,000 copies of his book. According to Nielsen BookScan data, Jacobson's novel sold 8,300 copies before winning the Man Booker. Being overall winner put the book on a different footing – as well as netting its author £50,000.

Becoming Award-Winning

So what is the best way to approach the award game? Should you deliberately set out to win prizes? I would argue that, if you are thinking about your literary career in a strategic way, then it makes perfect sense to try to raise your profile by entering as many competitions as you can. Even being a runner-up in a national competition is worthy of mention, and any endorsement of this kind will attract the attention of industry professionals and impress future readers.

On the other hand, don't get hung up about this. Your main goal must always be to write as much as you can, and as well as you can. Don't try to second-guess what any competition judges are looking for – this will almost certainly have an adverse effect on your work. There's a danger that the imagined voices of prize judges will become part of the white noise in your head. My own strategy is to write what I want to write, then see if my stories meet the guidelines of any relevant competitions. I have never written a short story or a novel with a specific award in mind, and I wouldn't recommend it.

The award-winning writer A. L. Kennedy takes a similar view. Her novel *Day* was named Costa Book of the Year in the Costa Book Awards in 2007 and in the same year she won the Austrian State Prize for European Literature. On her website she writes,

> I think the best theory to stick with would be that your best bet is to write as well as you can and enjoy that as much as possible and then – stop thinking about them, because they are not central to the job/vocation/arcane curse of being a writer. If you are accosted by prizes, that's a useful extra. Or you can network and chivvy and bargain and blackmail . . . I've seen that work, too. Depends who you want to be and how you want to live.
>
> As a judge of several I'm aware that some prizes are better organised than others, that some people care way too much about them and that often the book that comes second is the most interesting one. (You can use this to console yourself when you don't win and choose to believe there are exceptions to every rule when you do.)

The History of Fiction Prizes

Prizes for writing have a long history: the ancient Greeks handed out awards for poetry just as they did for athletics and other sports. But, after the classical period, writers vied for the attention and sponsorship of rich patrons, rather than the judges of prizes for literature. And, in the eighteenth and nineteenth centuries, the book business gave writers the chance to sell their wares directly to the reading public.

The first modern literary prize was established by Alfred Nobel, the inventor of dynamite. Before he died in 1896, he made a multimillion-dollar bequest to fund five international prizes for literature, chemistry, physics, medicine and peace. The first prizes were awarded in 1901, and the decisions were made by impartial committees, establishing the awards as being ethical and offering something like an objective standard of excellence. The first Nobel Prize in Literature was awarded to the French poet René (Sully) Prudhomme, and was covered by more than 100 newspapers across the world.

The success of the Nobel prize inspired imitators. The Goncourt and Femina prizes were set up in France in 1903 and 1905; the Pulitzer was launched in America in 1917; and in 1919 the James Tait Black Memorial prize was established in Britain. Not all the awards were for what was then known as 'highbrow' fiction. In 1955 the British Crime Writers' Association started awarding an annual prize for the best crime novel of the year; and other awards proliferated in the US and Europe.

But the biggest British award did not appear on the scene until 1968. Tom Maschler, an editor at Jonathan Cape, set up a new prize sponsored by the food company Booker Brothers. The Booker was designed to boost the profile of literary fiction by publicising a shortlist of authors, appointing high-profile judges and awarding the prize at a black-tie event.

The Booker gradually gained prestige and attracted more attention, and in 1981 it really hit the headlines when it was covered live on TV for the first time, and the award went to Salman Rushdie for *Midnight's Children*.

What is now the Man Booker Prize has been joined by a number of other UK prizes that can help a writer establish his or her name. These include the Costa Book Award (founded as the Whitbread in 1971), the Orange Prize (set up in 1996), the Samuel Johnson Prize (1999), the Wales Book of the Year (1992) and the Waverton Good Read Award (2003).

Know the Field

Be aware of these awards, read the trade press and the literary pages and see who is winning what and what judges appear to be looking for. But don't expect miracles – every competition is a lottery, and you will have to ask your publisher to enter you for the most important prizes. Writing in *Prospect* magazine, author Tom Chatfield comments,

> Winners can and do sell big, but no victory guarantees vast sales, and the tail-enders of shortlists often fare poorly. Most importantly – and despite the wishful claims of some publishers – there is still no substitute for word of mouth. In 2007, *The Reluctant Fundamentalist* by Mohsin Hamid lost out to Kiran Desai's *The Inheritance of Loss* in the Booker, but considerably outsold it, becoming one of the best-performing literary novels of the year (it was also, in my opinion, a far more ambitious and exciting book). Prizes grant opportunities, but their pronouncements remain at the mercy of the reading public.

Neither will winning a prize make it any easier to do the actual writing. As with all forms of attention from the outside world, a literary prize can be a distraction, making it harder to get back into the 'zone' and find the peaceful, secret inner place where good ideas come from and great writing is produced. After winning the Booker with *Life of Pi* in 2002, Yann Martel said 'all hell had broken loose' and he wrote nothing for eighteen months.

Hilary Mantel points out that winning the Booker means the pressure is on and expectations are greater. Writing in the *Guardian*, she commented,

> Even when you are taking your bow, lapping up applause, you do know this brute fact: that you are only as good as your next sentence. You might wake up tomorrow and not be able to do it. The process itself will not fail you. But your nerve might fail.

In other words, it is just as important to keep awards in perspective when you have won one as it is when you are still waiting for your Man Booker nomination. At the same time, in an overcrowded, insecure profession, being given an official seal of approval is good for both sales and morale.

How to be award-winning

I can't guarantee that you will win an award if you read this chapter, but I can promise that you will increase your chances if you do the following:

- Study the market. Become an expert in the literary award market, and research prizes that are relevant to your particular genre, such as crime, romance, sci-fi, fantasy, young adult.
- Write very short pieces specifically to enter competitions: flash fiction and micro fiction are gaining more attention.
- Write short stories and enter them for as many competitions as you can, rather than waiting for your novel to be finished, published and entered for the Man Booker.
- Read prizewinning books and stories. Don't try to copy

the style or content, but see what is current, and what is seen as cutting-edge and noteworthy by judges. Every book you read will help you develop your writing voice, and reading contemporary writing is particularly important, so this reading research will be doubly useful to you.

Awards

Novels

Authors' Club First Novel Award

The Authors' Club Best First Novel Award is awarded by the Authors' Club to the most promising first novel of the year, written by a British author and published in the UK during the calendar year preceding the year in which the award is presented. From its establishment in 1955, the prize has consistently picked out novelists who have gone on to have long and distinguished careers. Early winners included Brian Moore for *The Lonely Passion of Judith Hearne* and Alan Sillitoe for *Saturday Night and Sunday Morning*; other winners have included Paul Bailey, Gilbert Adair and Jackie Kay.

Authors' Club (at the Arts Club), 40 Dover Street, London W1S 4NP; 020 7408 5092; fax: 020 7409 0913; authors@ theartsclub.co.uk; http://dolmanprize.wordpress.com.

Betty Trask Prize

Betty Trask left a bequest to the Society of Authors in 1983 to fund a prize for first novels written by authors under the age of thirty-five in a romantic or traditional, but not experimental, style. The prize money, which totals £20,000, must be used for foreign travel. The prize is open to published and unpublished novels.

Betty Trask Prize (at the Society of Authors), 84 Drayton Gardens, London, SW10 9SB; 020 7373 6642; fax: 020 7373 5768; info@societyofauthors.org; www.societyof authors.org/betty-trask.

British Science Fiction Association Award – Best Novel

The BSFA awards are presented annually by the British Science Fiction Association, based on a vote of BSFA members and – in recent years – members of the British National Science Fiction Convention.

See www.bsfa.co.uk/BSFAAward.

Commonwealth Prize

The Commonwealth Writers' Prize is a leading award for fiction that was first awarded in 1987. The objectives of the prize are to promote new voices, reward achievement and encourage wider readership and greater literacy, thereby increasing appreciation of different cultures and building understanding between cultures. The Prize is organised and funded by the Commonwealth Foundation, and is supported by the Macquarie Group Foundation. Authors win £10,000 for the overall Best Book and £5,000 for the Best First Book.

Commonwealth Foundation, Marlborough House, Pall Mall, London, SW1Y 5HY; 020 7930 3783; fax: 020 7839 8157; www.commonwealthfoundation.com.

Costa Book Awards

Formerly known as the Whitbread Literary Awards, the Costas are one of the best-known literary prizes in the UK, recognising books by writers based in the UK and Ireland. There are five categories: First Novel, Novel, Biography, Poetry and Children's Book. The winner in each category receives £5,000. One of these five books is selected as the overall winner of the Book of the Year and receives a further £25,000, making a total prize fund of £50,000.

The Booksellers Association, Minster House, 272 Vauxhall Bridge Road, London SW1V 1BA; 020 7802 0802; fax: 020 7802 0803; info@costabookawards.com; www.costabookawards.com.

Galaxy National Book Awards

Known as the 'Nibbies', the Galaxy National Book Awards are a showcase for both popular and literary fiction. Both the awards ceremony and profiles of the winning authors are televised, and the producer is Amanda Ross of Cactus TV, formerly the producer of the 'Book Club' segment on Channel 4's *Richard & Judy*. Categories include: Sainsbury's Popular Fiction Book of the Year, More4 Non-Fiction Book of the Year and National Book Tokens New Writer of the Year. It's a competition that is upfront about the need to popularise good books, and attract corporate sponsorship to competitions. David Nicholls won the 2010 Popular Fiction Book of the Year award in the Galaxies, with *One Day* (Hodder & Stoughton).

Galaxy National Book Awards, PO Box 60, Cranbrook, Kent, TN17 2ZR; 01580 212041; fax: 01580 212041; nibbies@mdla.co.uk; www.galaxynationalbookawards.com.

Guardian *First Book Award*

The *Guardian* First Book Award was established in 1999 to reward the finest new literary talent with a £10,000 prize for an author's first book. The award is open to writing across all genres. It is unique among book awards as debut works of fiction are judged alongside those of non-fiction.

Literary Editor, *Guardian*, Kings Place, 90 York Way, London, N1 9GU; 020 3353 2000; books@guardian.co.uk; www.guardian.co.uk/books/guardianfirstbookaward.

IMPAC Dublin Literary Award

The International IMPAC Dublin Literary Award is the largest and most international prize of its kind. It involves libraries from all corners of the globe, and is open to books written in any language. The award, an initiative of Dublin City Council, is a partnership between Dublin City Council and IMPAC, a productivity improvement company, which operates in more than fifty countries.

International IMPAC Dublin Literary Award, Dublin City Library & Archive, 138–144 Pearse Street, Dublin 2, Ireland; +353 1 674 4802; fax: +353 1 674 4879; literaryaward@dublincity.ie; www.impacdublinaward.ie.

Man Booker Prize

The Man Booker Prize for Fiction, also known in short as the Booker Prize, is a literary prize awarded each year for the best original full-length novel written in the English language by a citizen of either the British Commonwealth or the Republic of Ireland. Winning the Man Booker Prize is the ultimate accolade for many writers. The winner of the prize receives an award of £50,000.

Colman Getty Consultancy, 28 Windmill Street, London WIT 2JJ; 020 7631 2666; fax: 020 7631 2699; info@colman-getty.co.uk; www.themanbookerprize.com.

Nobel Prize in Literature

The Nobel Prize in Literature is awarded by the Swedish Academy. The very first Nobel Prize in Literature was awarded in 1901 to the French poet and philosopher Sully Prudhomme, who in his poetry showed the 'rare combination of the qualities of both heart and intellect'. Over the years, the Nobel Prize in Literature has been awarded to the works of authors from many different languages and cultural backgrounds.

Swedish Academy, Box 2118, S-10313, Stockholm,

Sweden; +46 8 555 12554; fax: +46 8 555 12549; secretariat@svenskaakademien.se; www.nobelprize.org/nobel_prizes/literature.

Orange Prize for Fiction

The Orange Prize for Fiction celebrates women's writing. It is awarded annually for the best full-length novel by a female author of any nationality, written in English and published in the UK in the preceding year. It has become one of the most prestigious awards in the literary calendar. The winner receives £30,000, which is anonymously endowed, and a limited-edition bronze figurine called the 'Bessie' (also anonymously endowed).

Booktrust, Book House, 45 East Hill, London SW18 2QZ; 020 8516 2972/2960; fax: 020 8516 2978; tarryn@booktrust.org.uk; www.orangeprize.co.uk.

Short stories

BBC National Short Story Award

This is the largest award in the world for a single short story. A prize of £15,000 is awarded for the winning story, £3,000 for the runner-up and £500 for the three other shortlisted stories. In 2005, the National Short Story Prize was launched at the Edinburgh International Book Festival to re-establish the importance of the British short story after many years of neglect. It's funded by NESTA (the National Endowment for Science, Technology and the Arts) and supported by BBC Radio 4 and *Prospect* magazine. In 2008, the prize was renamed the BBC National Short Story Award to reflect the fact that the BBC is now the sponsor.

BBC, Room 316, BBC Henry Wood House, 3–6 Langham Place, London W1B 3DF; 020 7765 0121; rosa@booktrust.org.uk; www.theshortstory.org.uk/nssp.

Bridport Short Story Prize

The Bridport Prize International Creative Writing Competition was founded by Bridport Arts Centre in 1973 and has steadily grown in stature and prestige. Right from the start the competition attracted entries from all parts of the UK and from overseas. Today, many thousands of entries are received from more than 80 countries worldwide. The prize money and entry fees have risen over the years as well, and now the first prize in the poem and short-story categories is £5,000, second prize £1,000 and third prize £500. An additional ten supplementary prizes of £50, one for each category, are awarded. A new category for flash fiction with a prize of £1,000 was introduced in 2010.

Bridport Prize, PO Box 6910, Dorset, DT6 9BQ; 01308 423 888; frances@bridportprize.org.uk; www.bridportprize.org.uk.

Poetry

Forward Prizes for Poetry

The Forward Poetry Prizes were launched in 1991 to bring the public's attention to contemporary poetry. They are the richest annual awards in the UK, with a total prize value of £16,000, to reward both established and up-and-coming poets.

Forward Poetry Prize Administrator, Colman Getty Consultancy, 28 Windmill Street, London WIT 2JJ; 020 7631 2666; fax: 020 7631 2699; info@colmangetty.co.uk; www.forwardartsfoundation.org.

National Poetry Competition

Established in 1978, the Poetry Society's National Poetry Competition is one of the longest-running and most widely respected single-poem poetry competitions. Winning has given an important boost to a plethora of now widely known poets, including Poet Laureate Carol Ann Duffy and 2009 T. S.

Eliot Prize winner Philip Gross. It is judged anonymously by a new set of judges each year. The winning poems are published in *Poetry Review* and prizes are generous: the winner is awarded £5,000, the second prize is £2,000 and the third prize is £1,000.

Poetry Society, 22 Betterton Street, London WC2H 9BX; 020 7420 9880; fax: 020 7240 4818; info@poetrysociety.org.uk; www.poetrysociety.org.uk/content/competitions/npc.

Nonfiction

Orwell Prize

The Orwell Prize is the pre-eminent British prize for political writing. There are two annual awards: a Book Prize and a Journalism Prize. They are awarded to the book and for the journalism judged to have best achieved George Orwell's aim to 'make political writing into an art'. The prizes are intended to encourage writing and thinking in this tradition. The judges ask only that 'writing must be of a kind that is aimed at or accessible to the public, and submissions will be judged equally for the excellence of their style and the originality of their content'.

Media Standards Trust, 5/7 Vernon Yard, Portobello Road, London, W11 2DX; 020 7727 5252; gavin.freeguard@media-standardstrust.org; www.theorwellprize.co.uk.

Samuel Johnson Prize

The Samuel Johnson Prize celebrates diverse and thought-provoking writing in nonfiction. Sponsored by BBC4, it has been awarded since 1999. The prize covers current affairs, history, politics, science, sport, travel, biography, autobiography and the arts. The competition is open to authors of any nationality whose work is published in the UK in English.

Colman Getty Consultancy, 28 Windmill Street, London

WIT 2JJ; 020 7631 2666; fax: 020 7631 2699; info@colman-getty.co.uk; www.thesamueljohnsonprize.co.uk.

Children's fiction

Carnegie Medal

The Carnegie Medal is awarded annually to the writer of an outstanding book for children. It was established in 1936, in memory of the great Scottish-born philanthropist Andrew Carnegie (1835–1919). Carnegie was a self-made industrialist who made his fortune in steel in the USA. His experience of using a library as a child led him to resolve that 'if ever wealth came to me that it should be used to establish free libraries'. Carnegie set up more than 2,800 libraries across the English-speaking world and, by the time of his death, over half the library authorities in Great Britain had Carnegie libraries. The medal is awarded by CILIP, the Chartered Institute of Library and Information Professionals.

CILIP, 7 Ridgmount Street, London WC1E 7AE; 020 7255 0650; fax: 020 7255 0651; ckg@cilip.org.uk; www.carnegiegreenaway.org.uk/carnegie.

General

James Tait Black Memorial Prizes

The James Tait Black Memorial Prizes are Scotland's most prestigious and the UK's oldest literary awards, having been awarded since 1919. The prizes have achieved an international reputation for their recognition of literary excellence in biography and fiction. The two prizes, each of £10,000, are awarded annually, the prizewinners being chosen by the professor of English literature at the University of Edinburgh. Eligible works of fiction and biographies are those written in English, and first published or co-published in the United

Kingdom during the calendar year of the award. Writers of any nationality are eligible.

Department of English Literature, David Hume Tower, George Square, Edinburgh, EH8 9JX; 0131 650 3619; fax: 0131 650 6898; www.englit.ed.ac.uk.

John Llewellyn Rhys Prize

The John Llewellyn Rhys Prize rewards the best work of literature (fiction, nonfiction, poetry, drama) by a UK or Commonwealth writer aged thirty-five or under. This prize is awarded in honour of the writer John Llewellyn Rhys, who was killed in action in the Second World War. It was founded in 1942 by John Llewellyn Rhys's wife, also a writer, who began the award to honour and celebrate his life.

Booktrust, Book House, 45 East Hill, London SW18 2QZ; 020 8516 2972; fax: 020 8516 2978; tarryn@booktrust.org.uk; www.booktrust.org.uk.

For more information on writing prizes, go to www.bookprizeinfo.com or see *Writers' and Artists' Yearbook*.

Grants and Funding

As well as competitions, there are also a number of grants and funds for writers available in the UK. Your chances of a slice of this cake will not have been improved by recent government cutbacks, but, as with competitions, it is worth doing some research, finding out what you might be eligible for, and trying your luck. Grants may be given for research, to develop programmes, to fund various projects and theatrical plays, or simply to buy time to write. The two main sources of funding are the Arts Council and the Society of Authors, whose contact details – and those of other organisations – you can find in 'Useful Contacts'; awards funding can be found under 'Awards'.

The Arts Council

Grants for the arts in the United Kingdom and the Republic of Ireland are for activities carried out over a set period that engage people in artistic activities, and help artists and arts organisations in England carry out their work. As the author of a book, you are eligible for such an award. These grants are funded by the National Lottery. You can apply online or using a printed application form, but the Arts Council encourages applicants to use its online system to save on costs. The Arts Council also provides a 'how to apply' booklet, which explains exactly what you need to do to make an eligible application. Before you start, go to its website (www.artscouncil.org) and check out information on funding and eligibility. If you are eligible, you'll need to write a proposal about your book, as well as filling in an application form.

The Society of Authors

The Society of Authors is a nonprofit organisation founded in 1884 'to protect the rights and further the interests of authors'. It oversees numerous prizes, awards, funds and grants for writers who live in the UK. Grants administered by the organisation include the Authors' Foundation, which gives grants to authors who are working on projects for a British publisher. Grants are for help with the cost of research or for the author to be able to take time off to write. The Foundation does not give grants or awards to self-published authors.

The society also administers three charitable trusts, the Francis Head Bequest, the Authors' Contingency Fund and the John Masefield Memorial Trust. Grants are made to help with personal expenses in times of sudden financial crisis and are awarded only to professional authors who have earned a substantial amount of their income from writing. The

K. Blundell Trust is for British authors up to forty years of age who are working on a project for a British publisher. Funding is available for fiction and nonfiction works that aim to increase social awareness.

The Royal Literary Fund

The RLF is a benevolent fund set up to assist professional published authors who have suffered a loss of income and are having financial difficulties. The RLF also runs a fellowship for writers in partnership with British universities and colleges. This fellowship is also based on financial need.

Grants and Prizes: The Lowdown

- Grants and prizes are there for the taking. Don't wait to be asked – do your homework and find out what you are eligible for.
- Being awarded a prize at any stage in your career can make a huge difference to your status and your sales.
- Keep track of competitions, and keep sending out your writing. However, don't write with a specific award in mind – just do your best work.
- Although there have been cutbacks in arts funding, there are still grants and funding available for authors. Again, do your research.
- The two main funding bodies are the Arts Council and the Society of Authors, so it is fairly simple to find out what's available.
- Writing fellowships at universities are another possible route to funding. To find out more, contact the Royal Literary Fund.

The Last Word

I hope this book will be useful to you, both now and in the future. If I were to give a single piece of advice, it would be this: enjoy yourself. Take pride in what you do. Writing – and for most people that means fiction – is one of the greatest pleasures in life. (But don't let the idea of the Great Novel blind you to other forms of the written word, such as nonfiction, poetry and drama, all of which can be equally satisfying.) When you write, you take control of your thoughts, you pin down the passing moment, you begin to make sense of the turmoil in your mind. And, by telling stories, you are joining a host of others, now and throughout history, in this country and all over the world. Your words aren't products-in-waiting, validated only by publication. Your words are vital in themselves.

Your writing 'career' cannot and will not be a clear progression. There is no job design, no promotional hierarchy. Sometimes you will feel as if you are going backwards. Sometimes you will feel that nothing will ever happen again, it's just you, endlessly tapping on a keyboard for no reason. And sometimes you will feel as if you are the luckiest person in the world. You will win a competition. You will hold your newly published novel in your hands. A reader will notice something in your work that you didn't realise was there yourself. Or you will simply write a sentence, and read it back, and smile.

Good luck with it. Keep writing. Don't ever give up. But that's enough from me. I want to give another writer the last word . . .

A. L. Kennedy

A. L. Kennedy is a Scottish novelist, short-story writer, screen-writer and stand-up comedian. In 2003 she was nominated by Granta *magazine as one of twenty 'Best of Young British Novelists'. Among her novels is* Day *(2007), winner of the 2007 Costa Book of the Year Award; and a recent collection of short stories is* What Becomes *(2009). She also performs regularly – other commitments permitting – at the Wicked Wenches comedy evenings at the Stand Comedy Club in Glasgow.*

'I didn't always want to write because it was part of what I did from such an early age,' she says. 'It was like whistling or skipping or climbing trees – not that I was in any way good at doing any of those. But I didn't think I'd do them for a living, either.

'Being published at all was probably important – I know it felt good at the time. Then again, it involved almost no exposure in a tiny magazine and no money. Everything at the start was very low-key and low-income. I suppose moving to being self-employed and entirely freelance was a big deal, but, then again, I was still working flat out and not necessarily on what I'd wish, when I'd wish, so there wasn't that much real difference. There have been times when I've been aware of something moving, or being under more scrutiny – the first *Granta* Best of Young British Novelists listing, certainly winning the Costa – but those times are at least as uncomfortable as pleasant. There's never been a time when I've thought, Oh, I can have a rest now; oh, I've got enough cash to be secure; oh, I'm good at this.

'I see writing as telling stories about people to other

people, so nothing is really that separate from anything else. My advice is to try to keep on learning and to keep looking for stimulation – returning to good things, seeking out people who are excellent in their fields, or seeking out different aspects of yourself. Let your writing grow your life and let it be a way to live fully. But mainly, if you love it then find a way to do it – you only live once, why not go for it? If you stop loving it, then fix whatever's gone wrong or get out – it'll kill you otherwise.

'Writing for a living is a good way of enriching your life, by enriching others, by extending yourself for the benefit of strangers, giving them your best and your most beautiful – there's nothing wrong with that.

'But it will be hard. Beautiful and hard.'

APPENDIX A

Writing for Your Life

Quiz: Do You Have What it Takes?

OK, so you have come this far. You have read some, most or all of a book about how to be a writer. But will you act on the advice I have given you? Or will you fall by the wayside, like so many others? Take this quiz to find out how you measure up.

1. How many books have you read in the last month?

a. Four or more, of various genres and periods. You passionately love reading, books and words.

b. One improving tome. You have a list of '100 novels to read before I die' stuck on your pin board.

c. None. You want to be a writer, so there's no time to read as well.

d. You never read books.

2. How often do you write fiction/poetry/your journal?

a. Every day. It's like brushing your teeth.

b. Every week. Sunday morning is sacrosanct.

c. Every month. Well, nearly every month, anyway.

d. When the muse strikes. This is about genius, not jogging.

3. Which of the descriptions below best sums up your attitude to the act of writing itself?

a. An enjoyable challenge: there is no better way to clarify your thoughts and capture your ideas.

b. Hard work, but it's good to get it out of the way so you can focus on your marketing strategy.

c. Really boring, an exhausting chore.

d. Fantastic – when you have the time, every word you write is pure gold.

4. What is your ambition as a writer?

a. To publish a book that you are really proud of.

b. To be published at any cost.

c. To write a whole book, with chapter headings and everything.

d. To be J. K. Rowling.

5. What is your record on finishing what you started?

a. As long as you are sure you can do a good job, you will persevere when things get tough. You are dogged and meticulous.

b. You are obsessive and single-minded about any project that you care about. When you were seven, you built a matchstick model of Milton Keynes.

c. You stick at things until they get boring and frustrating. Life's too short.

d. You love new diversions, fads and hobbies! You can't wait to get this novel finished, and learn how to hang-glide!

6. If you are stuck or 'blocked' which of the following do you do?

a. Keep writing notes, but spend more time looking for inspiration at galleries, in the outside world or by listening to music. You have to feed your imagination sometimes.

b. Panic, bang your head on the computer keyboard, but keep going. Writing is not for wimps, and you will beat this.

c. Binge-drink. It worked for Hemingway, didn't it? Booze and creativity go hand in hand, like, well, booze and a hangover.

d. Curl up on the sofa with the box set of *Bridget Jones* or *The Godfather* and daydream. Anyway, you're not exactly stuck, because you haven't started yet.

7. Which of these descriptions best fits your attitude to rejection?

a. It always hurts, but you can't pursue any creative endeavour without hearing the word 'no' sometimes. So getting turned down is part of your professional life.

b. You scrutinise every rejection slip to see what the subtext is, and work out how to change your work accordingly.

c. Rejection stinks. They are bastards. There is a conspiracy out there. It's all about who you know or where you went to school.

d. Rejection? Who said anything about rejection? When you finally send your manuscript out, it will change the face of British publishing.

8. What's the best way to approach an agent?

a. Research the market, find out who is representing whom, and learn how to make a professional submission, tailoring each one to the individual agent.

b. Read the *Writers' & Artists' Yearbook* from cover to cover, taking notes and keeping a dossier on every agent in there. This is a military campaign.

c. Send out a standard letter to the first four agents that you fancy, and then try to think about something else.

d. Mail the best agent in the country the entire manuscript of your book, attached to a bouquet of red roses and a helium balloon, then sit back and wait for their call.

9. How long do you expect it will take to establish your career as a writer?

a. Years. You try to keep the momentum going, but this is not about overnight success.

b. Eighteen months. You have plotted your trajectory on a wall chart in your office.

c.   Who said anything about a career? Isn't this about Art and stuff?

d.   About three weeks. Or less. Starting from next Thursday.

10. What do you see as your greatest challenge?

a.   Keeping your writing fresh, exciting and original, and taking the time to edit and polish every draft till it is as good as it can possibly be.

b.   Staying abreast of what is going on in the publishing industry. So much going on, it's hard to make time for any actual writing.

c.   Filling up all those blank pages with words. *How* long do they say a novel is meant to be?

d.   Deciding whether to live in Los Angeles or New York when the Hollywood money starts rolling in.

11. What is your attitude to your day job?

a.   It's useful not only for earning a regular income, but also for keeping in touch with the real world, and getting ideas.

b.   You have worked out exactly how many hours you spend at work, and how many hours you spend asleep, factored in an equation covering mealtimes, commuting and watching *Grand Designs* and you still have 12.5 hours a week to write the novel.

c.   The people you work with are lovely. Sometimes, you spend the whole day chatting round the biscuit barrel and putting the world to rights.

d.   You are handing your notice in on Friday. No, Friday week.

12. What is 'Plan B'?

a.   That, no matter what happens, you will always be a writer. Writers are people who write, and you can never imagine doing anything else.

b.   You are working on an alternative publishing model. You have a full-scale model of the alternative publishing model in your garage.

c.   Whoa, steady on! You don't even have a 'Plan A' yet.

d. 'Plan B' is for losers. And you have a feeling you are going to be a winner.

How did you score?

Mostly a's

The Professional. You are idealistic enough to sustain yourself with the belief that writing is a worthwhile goal in itself, and realistic enough to know this is a challenging way to live your life. You approach writing in a balanced, mature way, knowing that you have to maintain your energy and motivation over years, not months. Above all, you know that this is not a game, and that, if you are going to be taken seriously by professionals in the publishing industry, then you have to behave like a professional yourself. No tantrums. No unrealistic goals. No messing. This attitude will not necessarily lead to fame and fortune, but it will enable you to keep writing – and, one day, who knows? The Booker prize could be yours. In the meantime, you know how to live in the present, and enjoy your writing life as it happens, rather than postponing your enjoyment of your craft till the day that your ambitions are realised.

Mostly b's

The Anorak. It may seem an odd thing to say in a 'how-to' book, but there is a chance that you are reading too many 'how-to' books. If so, make this the last one you buy. Writing well takes skill, application and attention to your craft, but you are over-complicating everything, and making the whole thing into home-work. Instead of making yourself a world expert on publishing, agents, market trends and who's who in the literary metropolis, try sitting down with your notebook for thirty minutes a day and letting the ideas flow. Remember that you cannot organise your literary career into existence. Some of it is down to chance. A lot will depend on the quality of what you write. Allow yourself to be open to new ideas, and let your right brain take over once in a while. Do this, and not only will you enjoy your writing life much more, but you might also write something that publishers will take seriously.

Mostly c's

The Dilettante. Now, be honest: have you read the rest of the book, or did you skip to this chapter because it was the shortest? And be even more honest: are you really, really determined to write? More determined than you are to lose that stubborn half-stone? Or go to the Maldives for your next holiday? Or take part in a triathlon? Because, on current form, writing is just another of your many hobbies. Want to change this? Then write every day, first thing in the morning if you can – and keep at it. Read on the train instead of texting. Apply yourself to this as if your life depended on it – because your life as a writer really does. Either that, or give up now, and get in training for that triathlon. You may be cut out to be in a writing group, or to write a few short stories when you retire, but you don't have what it takes to be a Writer.

Mostly d's

The Fantasist. If you carry on like this, the greatest work of fiction that you ever create will be the fantasy that you carry round in your head. That's right, the one where you win the Nobel prize and make a mountain of money, produce the greatest body of work since Shakespeare, are lionised, canonised and lauded across the planet – and probably on Mars and Jupiter as well. The brutal fact about being a writer is that it is really quite mundane. You need to take your craft seriously. You need to learn to do all the things that other writers learned to do before you. There are no shortcuts. There are no secrets. It's about the work. If you want to make your fantasy come true, then it's time to step out of your cloud and get on with it.

The good news

If you didn't score mostly a's and you find yourself languishing in one of the other categories, then join the club. We can all aim to be Professionals, but, actually, we are all human beings. Every writer has an inner Anorak, or is a part-time Dilettante or a frustrated Fantasist. And if we were all Professional, all the time, what a boring world it would be! Seek balance, and don't feel guilty if your writing personality, like your writing, is less than perfect.

Plan B

What do you do if every agent in London turns down your manuscript? What if you reach a point of utter exhaustion, when the rejection letters are pinned up all over your study wall, hemming you in with an endless 'No'? What do you do when you wake up at three o'clock in the morning and think, It is never going to happen? It is never, ever going to happen?

We writers tend to be a neurotic bunch, but repeated rejection is not good for anyone's self-esteem. Ultimately, if we hand the responsibility for our future happiness and peace of mind to the publishing industry, we may find that Prozac is not enough to keep us on the straight and narrow. You can be as professional and positive as you like, but, for a conventional publishing career to take off, you need the gatekeepers to let you in. If that doesn't happen, your dream of glittering success becomes a nightmare of permanent failure.

But there are two ways to lighten the mood. The gate keepers might be wrong. Your stubborn certainty that your books are more readable and relevant than half the Booker shortlist might be justified. The list of writers who were rejected time and time again is a long one, and includes both William Golding and J. K. Rowling. Even a writer like John Kennedy Toole was proved right in the end. Toole killed himself in despair after his book *A Confederacy of Dunces* was rejected by thirty-six publishers. Ten years after his death, his mother persuaded a publisher to print it. His 'unpublishable' novel became a cult success, and is now acknowledged as a classic of American comic fiction.

This may sound like a feeble compensation when your hopes have come to nothing. So here is the second mood-lifter. You can go it alone. You don't have to wait for someone else to wave a magic wand over your career, and give your books the chance to find an audience. The Internet is changing the face of global publishing, as we have seen, and one enormous, positive change that it has brought about for writers is the chance to write and publish at low cost, and to publicise their work to a community of potential readers. Self-publishing, which used to be hugely expensive and perceived as the last resort of the deluded and the narcissistic, is now respectable.

There is a different world out there now in terms of DIY printing. Cheaper digital publishing makes printing your own work more affordable, and the Internet makes self-publicity easier. But don't just rely on the Internet: you need to socialise as well. Go to events, introduce yourself to people and keep in touch with anyone you get on with. Facebook and other social media are good for following up contacts as well as making new ones. Live performances can also help sell your books. The poetry scene has really taken off, and young poets in particular are getting involved in public readings and performing at music festivals like Glastonbury.

The 'Do-it-Yourself' Career

Self-publishing of this kind has given many budding writers a platform. It's not to be confused with vanity publishing, which means that a company will publish an agreed print run of your book for you, usually for a large fee. A self-published book will have your name on the copyright page as the publisher, and you will need to register it with the ISBN Agency in your name as both author and publisher. Some self-publishers will publish your work from the file that you submit with very little interference, while others are very selective about what they publish in terms of content.

But they are generally much cheaper to use than a conventional vanity publisher because the print-on-demand facility – or POD, as it is known – means that overheads are much lower. *Writers' & Artists' Yearbook* suggests that you can expect to pay about £300 for 50 copies of a 150-page book without any pictures and from fully formatted files. It's essential to research the market thoroughly, but if you do your homework and plan this properly, you can ensure that your book does have a life as a printed artefact. Once you have done this, you then need to set about publicising your book.

The Local Scene

Apart from using a website, blog and social networking to publicise your work, you can also get a lot of mileage from making good contacts in your local areas. See Chapter 4 ('Networking') and Chapter 11 ('How To Be Your Own PR') for more ideas about this. Getting to know the movers and shakers in your area may feel like a challenge, but it's also enjoyable – and starting out is the hardest part. Once you are on the local radar, you will start being invited to events and hear about what's going on through word of mouth. Being part of the local community of writers in your area can also help boost your motivation and sense of purpose. Collaborations and live events such as readings and mini festivals are a great way to meet readers and get a direct response from an audience.

Setting up a writing circle

Another way of forging local links that are sustaining and inspiring is to set up a writing group – or join an existing one if possible. Starting out by joining a workshop is one way to begin, and you can then form an informal group with some like-minded students. Remember that you do need to have a good rapport with the other members, and that a workshop depends on mutual trust and respect between the various members.

Before you start, think about the time commitment you are about to make. Setting up your own writing group will mean that you have to attend most of the meetings and will also have to work behind the scenes, on such mundane tasks as administration and setting up the venue for the meeting. This takes time. You will also need to do a lot of reading – and a quick skim is not enough. Treat the work of your fellow writers with the respect that you would like to receive yourself. One approach is to run the group in a structured way, acting as group leader, offering advice and support to members and charging a small fee.

For more information on this, go to the website of the National Association of Writers' Groups (www.nawg.co.uk).

Writing as its Own Reward

Whatever you decide to do, my strong advice is to spend as much time as you can on writing if it gives you pleasure. The publishing industry is a business, and agents and publishers have no remit to make writers happy, or to publish work they don't think is commercial or professional enough. Don't let this ruin your life. Don't put your future on hold, waiting for that golden moment when you are finally allowed to become a Proper Writer. Anyone who writes regularly and with attention to their craft can claim this title as their own.

Ultimately, writing is its own reward. Meeting readers is wonderful. Talking to publishers and agents who 'get' your work is great. Seeing your book, fat and solid, sitting on a bookshelf is brilliant. But none of these things compare to the *doing* of it, the actual process of losing yourself in writing. This is the reality. This is what helps us make sense of our existence.

APPENDIX C

A Short History of Authors

'Times are bad. Children no longer obey their parents and everyone is writing a book.'   Cicero

Before Johannes Guttenberg invented the printing press in 1440, most people in Europe were illiterate. Books were handwritten and a rarity. Storytelling and singing were the only forms of entertainment available, and troubadours travelled from place to place, singing and performing courtly romances.

We have come a long way since those days – but earning a living from writing has never been easy or secure. In the earliest days of print, new plays and poems were listed at the Stationer's Hall in the City of London – an early form of registering copyright. Books and pamphlets were sold in bookshops or at travelling fairs. So the career of professional writer was born, with all its attendant neuroses and insecurities. Life wasn't easy for publishers, either. Public taste was unpredictable. Some would print grammars or law books for students, which were mandatory reading. If they were lucky, they would negotiate a patent from the Crown, giving them the sole right to publish almanacs or other occult guides. Then, as now, there was intense public interest in mysticism, violence and the bizarre. Most printers, like publishers today, had to make an informed guess about the likely success of a particular work, based on their experience and market knowledge.

Authors also had to contend with vitriolic responses from rival writers and the public at large. A published work was seen as fair game for attacks and negative criticism, and it was generally believed that, if an author was prepared to publish their work, they must take the consequences. Books and pamphlets, unless they were strictly theological, were regarded by religious zealots as 'the sermons of the devil'. And they certainly tended to be both populist and sensational. Keen to attract readers, printers would commission authors to write pamphlets that commented on dramatic topical events: natural disasters, one-eyed babies, plague outbreaks and other cataclysms.

Few writers got rich. William Shakespeare is an exception: but he was a 'sharer' in his theatre company, earning enough to buy property in Stratford. Others were less fortunate. One translator, Richard Robinson, has left detailed accounts behind him. Twelve of his books, printed over a period of fifteen years, earned him just £40 – a small amount even in the seventeenth century. He had to sell the lease of his house to make ends meet.

The New Profession

In 1710 the Copyright Act was introduced to benefit booksellers, who wanted the 'rights' to a particular piece of work to be signed to one particular seller. This was a form of patent, putting a work of fiction or poetry into a legal framework. Authors benefited, as it was recognised that the publisher was just the purchaser of a property that the author had originated. One of the first authors to take advantage of this was Alexander Pope, who negotiated good deals with booksellers and made a fortune out of his work translating Homer.

During the eighteenth century a new profession began to emerge: writers who produced both fiction and journalism. This was made possible by the rise of the periodical or magazine. Essay periodicals were also popular, publishing works by the likes of Daniel Defoe, who set up his own title, *The Review*. The most successful magazine of the eighteenth century was the *Gentleman's Magazine*, first published in 1732. Its contributors included Samuel Johnson, an archetypal English 'man of letters' who supplemented his income as an author with essays, reviews, news reports and articles.

Over this period, literacy was becoming more widespread and reading for pleasure was increasingly common. Magazines were cheap and circulating libraries lent out books for a small fee. London no longer dominated the market, and booksellers began to establish themselves in the provinces. By the end of the eighteenth century, the monopoly held by London booksellers had been broken, and books could be imported. Cheaper reprints followed, as well as the rise of a different breed of publisher. One of the earliest and most influential was John Murray II, the publisher of Jane Austen, Sir Walter Scott and Lord Byron.

In 1812 Murray published Byron's second book, *Childe Harold's Pilgrimage*, which sold out in five days, leading to Byron's observation 'I awoke one morning and found myself famous.' Unfortunately, Murray's decisions were not always sound. On Byron's death in 1824, Murray and five of the poet's friends tore up his memoirs and burned them in the fireplace at Murray's office. They believed the contents were so scandalous that they would damage Byron's reputation. (One lesson to learn from history is that luck plays a part in the survival of any manuscript. Exactly one hundred years later, when an obscure writer called Franz Kafka was dying of consumption in Prague, he asked his friend Max Brod to burn all his unpublished work. Brod ignored his friend's request, and published *The Trial*, *The Castle* and *Metamorphosis* to great acclaim.)

Victorian Publishing

Charles Dickens was another early publishing phenomenon. His career began when he was twenty-two, when he was commissioned to write a series of comic stories to illustrate a set of engravings. The finished book, *The Posthumous Papers of the Pickwick Club*, was published in twenty parts. Sales were slow to begin with, and the print run was reduced from 1,000 copies to 500. But then Dickens invented a new, humorous character called Sam Weller and *The Pickwick Papers* become a best-seller. Public appetite for Sam Weller stories gave rise to bootleg copies, theatrical performances and joke books.

The standard form of publishing in the nineteenth century was the three-volume novel. As books were expensive to produce, the idea was that Part One would whet the readers' appetite for Parts Two and Three. These volumes sold for 10s. 6d. (52.5p) – a substantial amount – but they could be loaned cheaply from the circulating libraries (such as Mudie's), which were privately owned. A three-part novel could make a librarian three times as much money as a single volume. The classic Victorian plot – complex and coincidence-strewn, with plenty of melodrama and then (most of) the loose ends tied up at the end – was perfect for this format. A three-volume novel was usually between 150,000 and 200,000 words long, and had forty-five chapters.

The publication of *The Pickwick Papers* not only marked the beginning of Dickens's career: it was also an early 'serial novel'. Publishing had become the first 'mass media' industry, and this made both publishers and authors rich – some of them, at least. As John Feather puts it in *A History of British Publishing*, 'In the nineteenth century, the vast increase in the output of the press created an army of writers and journalists who, unlike so many of their predecessors, could live by their pens. A successful author could expect rewards which put him among the best paid in the land.'

This was good news for both authors and their publishers, but, as the money rolled in, so did the potential for disagreement about who should take the larger slice of the profits. In particular, there were disputes about copyright. In the seventeenth century, writers were given a one-off payment; in the eighteenth century more complex arrangements developed, in which an author would typically be paid more if their work went into a second print run; while Sir Walter Scott insisted on sharing the profits of his work with the publisher equally, a practice copied by Dickens.

By the end of the nineteenth century, copyright law had been overhauled, and the law now allowed for the creation and protection of a complex web of rights. Adaptations, abridgements, serialisations and dramatisations all attracted their own rights. And, as profits rose, so did pressure. Publishers found themselves in a competitive market, and they needed a stream of new books to satisfy the demands of readers. Mudie's circulating library was increasing by anything up to 100,000 volumes a year, and authors were needed to produce new books. They were, therefore, in a stronger position than before.

The Society of Authors and the Net Book Agreement

While the likes of Dickens and Macaulay had plenty of bargaining power, middle-ranking authors had a tougher job on their hands. But it was their words that filled the columns of the monthly magazines and the three-volume books lent out by the circulating libraries. Out of this need the Society of Authors was formed. Alfred, Lord Tennyson, was the first president, and it soon established itself as a major force in the publishing world. In the 1890s, the society was involved in the negotiations that led to the signing of the Net Book Agreement.

The idea behind this new deal was that the author and the publisher would agree on terms, which effectively fixed prices. In theory, the author retained copyright, was paid 10 per cent of the net price of each copy sold, and retained the copyright and overseas and translation rights. But the exact terms varied. Then, as now, relations between authors and publishers were also variable, and could be tense. One thing is certain: by the end of the nineteenth century, publishing was a major British industry, worth millions of pounds. A published author was entering the world of business, whether they liked it or not.

The Rise of the Author's Agent

From the beginning, the agent was the go-between, who would negotiate on behalf of the author and help them through the complexities of a publishing contract. In return, they would take an agreed percentage of the author's income from any individual sale. (Usually this was 10 per cent.) The first agent to make a name for himself in England was A. P. Watt (1834–1914), who set up in business as an agent in 1875 after working in publishing and bookselling.

Agents wanted to get the best possible deal – the higher the fee, the higher their percentage – and were also motivated to see that manuscripts were delivered to publishers on time and in good order. They knew the market, so could direct an author to the publishing house most likely to be interested in their work, and a new author could use the name of a well-known agent as their endorsement. This increased the professionalism of the industry.

Mass-Market Publishing

During the twentieth century, there was enormous social upheaval in Britain, reflected by both the content of books and the way in which they were sold. Change came in the second half of the century, with greater influence from American publishing houses and eventually mergers and the formation of global publishers. But one of the most important changes of the early part of the century was the arrival of paperback publishing, led by Allen Lane, who set about publishing ten 'Penguin' titles in paperback format, with the aim of selling them in chain stores. Confident that good books could be sold in large numbers, he set the price at sixpence (2.5p). And he published a varied list, which included books by Compton Mackenzie, Dorothy Sayers and Ernest Hemingway.

The Penguin approach was relatively highbrow, but the mass-market revolution that followed changed the publishing industry on both sides of the Atlantic. Paperbacks sold in vast numbers. In 1985, some 48 million mass-market paperbacks were produced in Britain, generating a turnover of more than £40 million. They were sold in newsagents and at railway stations and airports. By the end of the 1970s, these outlets were responsible for about 20 per cent of all book sales in Britain.

The publishing houses themselves were also about to go through a major upheaval. Until the 1960s, the major London publishing houses had not essentially changed much for forty or fifty years. They were based in central London – usually Bloomsbury – and had a very clear idea what sorts of houses they were, and what sorts of books they wanted to publish. A key factor in this was that they were small enough to have a shared ethos that staff instinctively understood. Many were still family businesses, and most published fewer than a hundred titles a year.

Publishing Today

The 1980s and 1990s saw a pattern of mergers and acquisitions in the publishing world, with many of the established names that had dominated British publishers swallowed up by global players. Of the major houses that dominated the scene till the 1980s, only Faber and Faber remains independent. Other, newer independent houses like Canongate, Tindal Street and Atlantic Books are doing well. (All of them operate under the umbrella of the Independent Alliance.) But a market that is dominated by the likes of Pearson and Hachette Livre prefers to deal with large customers and large volumes of books. They are not interested in small, independent retailers or limited print runs. The collapse of the Net Book Agreement in 1997 led to competition on price between high street retailers, and cut-price offers from Amazon and other online retailers. This made it harder for authors, agents and publishers to survive unless they were producing best-selling books, printed in large quantities and making significant profits.

One thing remains clear: there are millions of literate people in

Britain, with leisure time to fill. Not all of them will read books. Not all books will be read in paper format. Film, TV and gaming will take the place of reading for a significant number. Even so, the world population is increasing, the ageing population in the West is growing and in a global publishing market, with English spoken as a lingua franca across the world, there are millions of people who might read your work.

And, whatever else has changed, there is one aspect of a writer's life that has changed little since the days when travelling troubadours sang for their supper. The market may shift and falter, the means of reaching readers may be influenced by technical innovations from the printing press to Kindle, but the appetite for a good story remains.

Useful Contacts

UK and Ireland

Society of Authors
84 Drayton Gardens
London SW10 9SB
020 7373 6642
www.societyofauthors.org
info@societyofauthors.org

Writers' Guild of Great Britain
15 Britannia Street
London WC1X 9JN
020 7833 0777
fax: 020 7833 4777
www.writersguild.org.uk
admin@writers-guild.org.uk

Arts Council England
14 Great Peter Street
London SW1P 3NQ
Postal enquiries to:
National Service Centre
The Hive
49 Lever Street
Manchester M1 1FN
0845 300 6200
fax: 0161 934 4426
www.artscouncil.org.uk
chiefexecutive@artscouncil.org.uk

Arts Council/An Chomhairle Ealaion
The Arts Council, 70 Merrion Square
Dublin 2
+353 1 6180200 / +353 1 676 1302
www.artscouncil.ie
enquiry form on website

Arts Council of Northern Ireland
77 Malone Road
Belfast BT9 6AQ
028 9038 5200
fax: 028 9066 1715
www.artscouncil-ni.org
info@artscouncil-ni.org

Arts Council of Wales
Bute Place,
Cardiff CF10 5AL
0845 8734 900
fax: 029 2044 1400
www.artswales.org.uk
info@artswales.org.uk

Creative Scotland (formerly the Scottish Arts Council)
12 Manor Place
Edinburgh
and
249 West George Street
Glasgow G2 4QE
0845 603 6000
www.creativescotland.com
enquiries@creativescotland.com

Authors Licensing and Collecting Society
The Writers' House
13 Haydon Street
London EC3N 1DB
020 7264 5700
fax: 020 7264 5755
www.alcs.co.uk
alcs@alcs.co.uk

British Council (London)
10 Spring Gardens
London SW1A 2BN
020 7389 4385 (8 a.m.–6 p.m.) /
020 7839 6347 (other times)
www.britishcouncil.org
enquiries@britishcouncil.org

British Council (Manchester)
Bridgewater House
58 Whitworth Street
Manchester M1 6BB
0161 957 7000
fax: 0161 957 7762
www.britishcouncil.org
enquiries@britishcouncil.org

Directory of Writers' Circles, Courses and Workshops
Diana Hayden
39 Lincoln Way
Harlington LU5 6NG
(the directory publishes a list of writers' circles, writing courses and
workshops throughout the UK)
01525 873 197
www.writers-circles.com
diana@writers-circles.com

PEN International
Brownlow House,
50–51 High Holborn
London WCIV 6ER
020 7405 0338
www.internationalpen.org.uk
info@internationalpen.org.uk

English PEN Centre
6–8 Amwell Street
London EC1R 1UQ
020 7713 0023
www.englishpen.org
enquiries@englishpen.org

Royal Literary Fund
3 Johnson's Court
London EC4A 3EA
020 7353 7159
www.rlf.org.uk
egunnrlf@globalnet.co.uk

Royal Society of Literature
Somerset House
Strand
London WC2R 1LA
020 7845 4676
www.rslit.org

Writers in Prison Network
PO Box 71
Welshpool
SY21 0WB
01938 810402
www.writersinprisonnetwork.org
wipn@btinternet.com

Literary consultancies

Cornerstones
Milk Studios
34 Southern Row
London W10 5AN
020 8968 0777
www.cornerstones.co.uk
kathryn@cornerstones.co.uk
helen@cornerstones.co.uk

Literary Consultancy
Free Word Centre
60 Farringdon Road
London EC1R 3GA
020 7324 2563
www.literaryconsultancy.co.uk
info@literaryconsultancy.co.uk

Writers' Workshop
7 Market Street
Charlbury OX7 3PH
0845 459 9560
www.writersworkshop.co.uk
info@writersworkshop.co.uk

Writing Coach
www.thewritingcoach.co.uk
jacqui@thewritingcoach.co.uk

Awards

For awards, see individual addresses under 'Awards' in Chapter 14.

Australia

Australian Society of Authors
PO Box 1566
Strawberry Hills NSW 2012
(+61) 2 9318 0877
www.asauthors.org
asa@asauthors.org

Writers' centres

NSW Writers' Centre
PO Box 1056
Rozelle NSW 2039
02 9555 9757
www.nswwriterscentre.org.au
info@nswwc.org.au

Sydney Writers' Centre
Ground Floor
55 Lavendat Street
Milsons Point NSW 2061
02 9929 0088
www.sydneywriterscentre.com.au
courses@spendriftmedia.com.au

Queensland Writers' Centre
Level 2, State Library of Queensland
Cultural Centre, Stanley Place
South Bank Q4101
07 3842 9922
www.qwc.asn.au
gldwriters@gwc.asn.au

Victorian Writers' Centre
Level 3, The Wheeler Centre
176 Little Lonsdale Street
Melbourne VIC 3000
03 9094 7855
http://vwc.org.au

The Tasmanian Writers' Centre
First Floor, Salamanca Arts Centre
77 Salamanca Place
Hobart
03 6224 0029
www.tasmanianwriters.org
admin@tasmanianwriters.org

New Zealand

The New Zealand Society of Authors
PO Box 7701
Wellesley Street
Auckland 1141
(+64) 9 379 4801
www.authors.org.nz

Writing organisations

International Writers' Workshop
PO Box 36652
Northcote
Auckland 0748
www.iww.co.nz

New Zealand Book Council
Stephenson & Turner House
156–158 Victoria Street, Te Aro
Wellington 6011
+64 4 801 5546
www.bookcouncil.org.nz

New Zealand Writers Guild
PO Box 47 886
Ponsonby
Auckland 1144
+64 9 360 1408
www.nzwritersguild.org.nz
info@nzwg.org.nz

South Africa

South African Writers' Network (SAWN)
PO Box 2720
6170 Eastern Cape
+27 (0) 46 624 2793
www.sawn.co.za

South African Writers' Circle
PO Box 2342
Westville 3630
fax: 031 564 2059
http://sawriters.org.za

Further Reading

Nonfiction

The Agony and the Ego, Clare Boylan (Penguin, 1993)
A collection of interviews with writers talking about the stresses and strains – and joys – of the creative process.

Enemies of Promise, Cyril Connolly (Penguin, 1961)
Advice to a young writer, including a history of literary trends and a dire warning about the threat to promise of 'the pram in the hall'.

From Pitch to Publication, Carole Blake (Macmillan, 1999)
This book focuses specifically on the publication process and gives an invaluable insider view – from the point of view of one of London's best known agents.

The Handbook of Creative Writing, edited by Steven Earnshaw (Edinburgh University Press, 2007)
A detailed handbook that is academic in tone – useful as a resource, with the focus on the craft of writing.

How to Lose Friends and Alienate People, Toby Young (Abacus, 2002)
Columnist and former co-editor of the *Modern Review* goes to New York in search of world domination, and finds humiliation – which boosts his profile.

A Life's Work: On Becoming a Mother, Rachel Cusk (Fourth Estate, 2002)

The story of Cusk's pregnancy and the birth of her first child, following the ups and downs of the early months of motherhood.

The Long Tail: Why the Future of Business is Selling Less of More, Chris Anderson (Hyperion, 2008)
Influential book looking at the power of niche marketing using the Internet to find your market.

A Novel in a Year, Louise Doughty (Simon & Schuster, 2007) and *On Writing,* Stephen King (New English Library, 2001)
These are two of the most widely read 'how-to' books on the market. Both focus on the craft of writing, and offer advice and words of wisdom about all stages of the creative process.

Outliers, The Story of Success, Malcolm Gladwell (Penguin, 2009)
Essays about the secret of success: intelligence, luck, cultural context and hard work (those essential 10,000 hours).

Plug Your Book: Online Marketing for Authors, Steve Weber (Weber Books, 2007)
Jargon-free guide to marketing your books online, with special mention of using Amazon.

A Room of One's Own, Virginia Woolf (Mariner Books, 1989)
Essay by Virginia Woolf, first published in 1929. Woolf talks about the status of women, and women artists and famously insists that a woman must have money and a room of her own if she is to write.

The Right to Write, An Invitation and Initiation into the Writing Life, Julia Cameron (Tarcher, 1999)
Personal essays and exercises (many of them adapted from her earlier best-seller *The Artist's Way*), which are designed to help readers enjoy writing. 'All of us have a sex drive. All of us have a drive to write.'

This is Your Brain on Music: Understanding a Human Obsession, Daniel J. Levitin (Atlantic Books, 2008)
An investigation of the power and effect of music, for which Levitin draws on his background as a musician and scientist.

Tribes, Seth Godin (Piatkus, 2008)
Godin argues that, for the first time, everyone has an opportunity to start a movement – to bring together a tribe of like-minded people and find their 'tribe'.

Writers' & Artists' Yearbook (A & C Black Publishers)
The reference book that no serious writer or would-be writer should be without. It is also worth investing in a new copy each year, as names and contact details change quickly in the current publishing market.

Writers' & Artists' Yearbook Guide to Getting Published, Harry Bingham (A & C Black Publishers, 2010)

Writing for Multimedia and the Web, Timothy Paul Garrand (Focal Press, 2006)
Information on the written word and its relationship to the Internet.

Your Writing Coach: From Concept to Character, from Pitch to Publication, Jurgen Wolff (Nicholas Brealey Publishing, 2007)
Wolff's book focuses on the writing process and the inner life of the writer, and his USP is that he is a motivational coach.

History of Writing

English Books & Readers: Being a study in the history of the book trade in the reign of Elizabeth I, H. S. Bennett (Cambridge University Press, 1965)

A Short History of British Publishing, John Feather (Routledge, 2006)

Fiction – Books About Being a Writer

Angel, Elizabeth Taylor (Virago, first published 1957)
Angelica ('Angel') Deverell is the wilful, lonely, misguided author of sensational romances. Taylor tells her life story, from adolescence until old age and death. Wealthy and famous, she is still somehow trapped by her own books, and her fantastical view of the world isolates her from everyone around her. A brilliant depiction of the author as a tragic and monstrous figure, based on the lives of romantic novelists Maria Corelli and Ethel M. Dell.

Atonement, Ian McEwan (Jonathan Cape, 2001)
Piqued by rejection, Briony Tallis tells a terrible lie, which comes to haunt her for the rest of her life. Her invented story ruins the life of both her sister Cecilia and her sister's lover Robbie. As an adult, she seeks atonement for her transgression by writing about it – which leads to an exploration on the nature of truth and fiction.

The Crack-Up, F. Scott Fitzgerald (New Directions, 1945)
This posthumous collection of essays sheds light on Fitzgerald's descent from glamorous poet of the Jazz Age to alcohol-soaked middle age and premature death. He links his own hubris and crazed consumption with that of America, and this collection is both beautifully written and a warning to the young and vain.

Experience, Martin Amis (Vintage, 2000)
Amis's memoir covers a lot of ground, including the murder of his cousin Lucy Partington, but its most memorable sections concern his robustly dysfunctional relationship with the Old Devil himself, his father Kingsley. Their writing seemed to form not a bond, but a barrier between them – an insight worth bearing in mind if you think writing will resolve any family issues you may have.

The Golden Notebook, Doris Lessing (Michael Joseph, 1962)
Lessing's influential novel deconstructs the life of Anna Wulf, a former Communist living in postwar London with her young daughter. She writes four notebooks: 'a black notebook which is to do with Anna Wulf the writer; a red notebook concerned with politics; a yellow notebook, in which I make stories out of my experience; and a blue notebook which tries to be a diary'.

Keep the Aspidistra Flying, George Orwell (Victor Gollancz, 1936)
Gordon Comstock gives up his job in advertising and takes a low-paid job in a bookshop in order to pursue his career as a poet, and work on his magnum opus *London Pleasures*. But events conspire against him: he gets his girlfriend pregnant and eventually gives up on poetry, throwing his precious manuscript down a drain and returning to his advertising job.

Misery, Stephen King (Viking, 1987)
Novelist Paul Sheldon is injured after a car crash and held captive by Annie, a psychotic fan, in her isolated home. He has killed off her favourite character, Misery Chastain, and she wants him to

write a new novel in which Misery returns, but she goes to extraordinary and, for him, painful lengths to achieve her wish.

My Brilliant Career, Miles Franklin (William Blackwood & Sons, 1901)
Imaginative, headstrong Sybylla Melvyn dreams of being a writer, but is stuck in rural Australia in the 1890s. Convinced that she is ugly, she rejects a proposal from a wealthy suitor and decides she will never marry. The novel ends with no suggestion that she will ever have the 'brilliant career' that she craves.

New Grub Street, George Gissing (Brewster, 1891)
The story of two very different Victorian men of letters: Edwin Reardon, idealistic and determined to write a great novel, and Jasper Milvain, a worldly young journalist who networks with the right people and despises his clients. Reardon believes Art is more important than Mammon, and suffers the consequences.

The Old Devils, Kingsley Amis (Random House, 1986)
Alun Weaver, novelist and professional Welshman, returns to Wales as an elderly man, and takes up with his old friends. Soon after his arrival he drops dead. However, his return has sent shock waves through the close but competitive group.

Paper Men, William Golding (Faber and Faber, 1984)
The dark tale of a successful but alcoholic writer, Wilfred Barclay, and his struggle with his would-be biographer Rick Tucker, a young academic. Their fight over Barclay's personal papers – the symbol of his life – is both comic and desperately sad. Another sharp, painful glimpse into the life of a successful author.

Index